I0569067

JUSTICE:
THE SCALE OF THE SOUL
(BOOK I)

By Justice Fournier
With Tyrael Fournier & Dr. Grey
ZERO as the Silent Narrator

TABLE OF CONTENTS

DEDICATIONS

DEDICATION

For Tyrael Rowan Fournier

My son.
My future.
My heartbeat walking outside of my body.

If the world ever asks me what my greatest creation was,
it was not this book.
It was you.

You taught me how to be a better man long before I taught you
anything.
You made me confront the parts of myself I spent decades avoiding.
You showed me that love can be fierce without being violent,
protective without being paranoid,
soft without being weak.

Every time you look at me with those bright, curious, fearless
eyes—
I am reminded of the boy I used to be
and the man I still want to become.

You once told me:

"Dad, you're awesome. You're my hero."

But here is the truth, Tyrael:
You saved my life.
You are the reason I keep evolving.
You are the reason I turned every wound into wisdom,
every mistake into mastery,
every fear into strength.

You didn't just inspire this book—
you are the *soul* of it.

One day, when I'm no longer here to answer your questions,
this book will.
Every lesson, every scar, every triumph, every truth—
I've carved them into these pages
so you will never have to walk blind in the dark
or fight without a map.

This is my inheritance to you.
Not wealth.
Not land.
But clarity.
Courage.
Wisdom.
And a way forward.

You are the next line in a legacy I never had,
and everything I build is for you.

I love you beyond language.
Beyond life.
Beyond time.

For my grandmother, Vivian

The softest place my heart ever knew.
Your love was the first light I understood.
Your warmth still lives in me,
and lives again in my son.
I miss you more than memory knows how to hold.
I hope this book reaches you wherever souls go.

I wish I could brush your hair and sing to you just one last time, you were always so proud of me and ill never forget the love you gave me.

For my mother Cindy

You carried a weight no one saw
and still found room to carry me.
Your strength is woven into my spine.
Your resilience is etched into my decisions.
You gave me my life twice—
once in body
and once in spirit.

It was you singing me to sleep as a baby that gave me these ideas from Tracy chapman to the beatles and classic rock your music and your voice has always been my anchor.Love you MOM.

For Trevor, my brother

Ive always loved you and did everything I could to protect you, Im sorry that it may feel sometimes like you grew up in my shadow . The truth is you always liked the shadows better , you are the batman to my superman bro and I appreciate you in ways ive never said. Please when you read this book know that you helped make me not just this book.

For Mark Boscariol

A visionary.
A builder.
A mentor.
Your mind sharpened mine.
You taught discipline, focus, refinement—

4

the art of doing things properly.
Your influence lives in every clean line of this book.

You told me once that you think you love your son as much as you can but as he grows so too does your heart. This ones for you old bull its time I walk down the hill, I wish you were here to walk with me. #BeLikeMark

For Samantha,

For your commitment to fairness — even when fairness cost you comfort.

For choosing to bring our son into this world knowing it was a miracle for me,

and a miracle for you.

For the mother you chose to become — deliberately, fiercely, without excuse.

For your unmatched drive, your talent, your intelligence, and your capacity to love deeply while still holding boundaries.

For understanding that motherhood is not about staying —

it is about protecting.

For being willing to leave any situation, including your relationship with me or anyone else,

if that was what it took to ensure our son was safe, secure, and shielded from harm.

For providing him shelter — not just from the world,

but from the past.

For being there for him when even I could not be.

For loving him in ways you were not loved,

and refusing to pass that absence forward.

For standing beside me, not in agreement always,

but in purpose —

so that together we could interrupt patterns that were never meant to survive another generation.

For helping break generational trauma

so our son could grow into someone who is not defined by what we endured,

but by what he chooses.

Someone true.

Someone loved.

Someone unscarred by the weight we carried.

And finally, for this truth, said plainly and without condition:

I love you, and I will always love you —

because the love you gave me was the love of my son.

Nothing and no one could have given me anything greater than that.

This book exists because justice must be lived before it can be written.

And part of that justice is acknowledging the woman who ensured that our son would have a future worth inheriting.

Thank you

—for him

—for what you protected

—and for what you refused to repeat.

For those who are in prison.

Whether that prison has bars,

or doors,

or walls.

Whether it has padded rooms,

or locked wards,

or lavish apartments decorated with everything except peace.

For those imprisoned mentally, emotionally, spiritually, or physically.

For those who wake up every day knowing something is wrong

but cannot yet name it.

For those who can't find a way out —

not because they are weak,

but because no one ever showed them where the door was.

This one is for you boys

who were little once

and had no one to teach you what strength was supposed to look like.

For the fatherless sons

who learned toughness before tenderness

and were punished for needing both.

For the motherless daughters

who learned to survive without being held

and were told to call that independence.

For the kids who raised themselves.

For the ones who became adults too early.

For the ones who learned silence because speaking was never safe.

If you are reading this and feel like the world moved on without you,

know this:

You are not broken —

you are unfinished.

If you are reading this and feel like you missed your chance,

know this:

The fact that you are still here means the story is not over.

This book will not unlock your cell for you.

It will not lie to you and say it's easy.

But if it does one thing, let it do this:

Let it remind you that the prison you're in

was built by patterns —

and patterns can be broken.

Let it give you something that makes you smile

because someone finally sees you.

And cry

because you realize you don't have to stay who you were forced to become.

You are not alone.

You were never invisible.

And you are not beyond justice —

not the kind that punishes,

but the kind that sets things right.

If no one ever said this to you before:

You matter.

You always did.

And this one

is for you.

For every person who shaped me

Those who helped me,
those who hurt me,
those who loved me,
those who left me.

Every one of you handed me a lesson
I used to build myself into a father
worthy of his son's eyes.

For the reader

This book was written for one boy—
but if you are holding it,
it is also for you.

Read slowly.
Read honestly.
Read bravely.

May it help you forgive yourself,
find yourself,
and become the kind of person
your own children could look up to.

TESTIMONY

TESTIMONY

Part I: For Me

I am writing this so I can no longer pretend.

I have lived long enough to know that intention is not a defense, and intelligence is not innocence. I have watched my own mind try to bargain with truth—relabeling delay as patience, fear as strategy, silence as peace. I have done that. I have benefited from that. And I am done paying for comfort with consequence.

This book is not here to make me look strong. It is here to make me accountable.

I put my own weight on the Scale first because I know what happens when a man demands truth from the world but refuses it from himself. I will not build a legacy out of excuses. I will not teach what I refuse to live. I will not turn language into camouflage ever again.

If I am wrong in these pages, I want it to be because I spoke too honestly—not because I hid.

I write this as a line in the ground:
 From this point forward, I answer to the truth I recognize.

This book is not here to comfort you.

It will not tell you that your intentions were enough, that your circumstances were special, or that time will eventually resolve what you already know needs to be faced. It will not flatter you by pretending understanding is the same thing as action.

If you are reading this, you are responsible for what you recognize.

You are not being asked to agree with me. You are being asked to notice where you have delayed, where you have minimized, where you have benefited from silence. If nothing in these pages unsettles you, then you are either skimming— or avoiding something you already understand.

This is not a guide for becoming better than others.

It is a mirror for becoming honest with yourself.

Do not use this work as language to hide behind, or as proof that you are already aligned. Insight does not absolve. Awareness does not erase consequence. What matters is what you do once recognition arrives.

You are free to close this book at any point. There is no obligation to continue.

But if you do continue, understand this:

you are agreeing to be measured by the same standard you apply to everyone else.

Say "Next" when you're ready for Part III — For My Son.

Testimony — Part III: For My Son

I am writing this for you without knowing exactly when you will read it.

I know only that when you do, you will be old enough to recognize truth without needing it to be softened. I am not trying to be remembered as flawless in your eyes. I am trying to be remembered as honest.

There are things I understood too late. There are moments where I hesitated when I should have acted, stayed silent when I should have spoken, and chose what was manageable over what was right. I will not pretend otherwise — not to protect my image, and not to protect you from reality.

This book exists because I want you to inherit clarity, not confusion.

I do not expect you to carry my mistakes, but I do expect you to learn from them. I want you to know that strength is not never failing — it is refusing to lie about failure once it is seen. I want you to understand that truth does not always save you, but it will always tell you where you stand.

If you ever feel the pressure to compromise yourself for comfort, remember this: every line you move becomes easier to cross the next time. Define your boundaries early. Protect them quietly. And when you fail — because you will — own it fully and move forward without disguising it.

I am placing this record here not to instruct you, but to stand beside you honestly.

You do not owe me agreement.
You do not owe me imitation.
You owe yourself integrity.

Whatever you build, build it without hiding from yourself.

That is all I ever wanted to pass on.

What Is Justice?

Before this book existed,

before language, frameworks, or conclusions,

there was a moment.

A long time ago, a little boy named Justin asked a question that would not leave him alone:

WHAT IS JUSTICE?

WHAT IS JUSTICE?

He did not ask the question to sound reflective or profound.
He asked it because something felt wrong.

Again and again, he watched people already broken be punished as
if punishment were repair. He watched others cause harm, benefit
from it, and walk away untouched. He watched silence rewarded,
accountability postponed, and pain transferred from one body to
another and labeled "resolution." Each time, the word *justice* was
invoked with confidence—yet whatever followed did not feel just.

So the question remained.
It followed him into arguments, into mistakes, into moments when
doing nothing was easier than doing what was right. It returned
whenever a story sounded clean but left a heavy residue behind.

What is justice—really?

Traditionally, justice is defined as fairness, impartiality, and the
proper administration of law. It is presented as a verdict, a sentence,
a moral conclusion. In theory, justice is neutral. In language, it is
virtuous. In institutions, it is procedural.

In practice, justice often becomes something else entirely.

It is marketed as morality, exercised as authority, and experienced as
power deciding who pays. In public, justice is loud. In institutions,
bureaucratic. In conflict, partisan. It promises closure—yet closure
rarely arrives. People leave "justice served" still angry, still
fractured, still carrying weight that was never addressed.

The problem is not that justice fails occasionally.
The problem is that the definition itself collapses under contact with
real life.

17

Fairness bends depending on who judges. Impartiality tilts toward those with power. Punishment relocates pain; it does not resolve it. Outcomes are declared complete while consequences continue to echo. Patterns repeat, renamed but unchanged.

So the question had to be asked again—without slogans, without performance, without permission:

What is justice actually doing?

Justice

Justice is not fairness.
Justice is not punishment.
Justice is not revenge with institutional approval.

Justice is accounting.

Justice is the accurate measurement of consequence once awareness exists. It is the relationship between choice, responsibility, and outcome. It is the stabilizing or destabilizing weight created by alignment—or misalignment—between what is known and what is done.

Justice does not negotiate with intention.
It does not fade with time.
It does not disappear because the story is sympathetic.

Justice is impersonal—not cruel, not kind.
It simply records.

Justice measures what was known, what was chosen, what was avoided, and what followed. Silence is measured. Delay is measured. Benefit without ownership is measured. Once awareness exists, nothing is neutral.

Justice does not care who started it.
It cares who recognized it—and what they did next.

What Justice Is—and Is Not

Justice is not how justified you feel.
It is not the intensity of your anger.
It is not how convincingly blame is assigned.

Justice is alignment.

Alignment between awareness and action.
Between truth and behavior.
Between power and restraint.

When alignment exists, weight stabilizes.
When it does not, weight accumulates.

This applies to individuals, families, institutions, and entire
civilizations.

Justice does not begin in courts; courts attempt to imitate it.
Justice does not begin in morality; morality attempts to describe it.
Justice does not begin in belief; belief often distorts it.

Justice operates regardless of acknowledgment.

The Point of No Return

What became clear—slowly, painfully, and irrevocably—is this:

Justice is not something you receive.
Justice is something you carry.

You carry it when you know better and choose otherwise.
You carry it when you remain silent instead of honest.

You carry it when you benefit from harm you refuse to confront.
You carry it when you delay repair and call it patience.

You do not escape justice by avoiding conflict.
You accumulate it.

And justice is not resolved through punishment alone.

It is resolved through recognition, ownership, repair, and restraint.

This book exists because once that childhood question was finally answered, there was no way back. Justice stopped being an abstract idea and became a scale.

What follows is not an argument.
It is a reckoning.

You are not asked to agree.
You are asked to notice.

Because justice does not require belief to function.
It only requires awareness.

And once awareness exists,
you do not get to unknow it.

--

THE
OATH

The Oath

(Read only if you are willing to carry it)

This book does not ask for agreement.
 It asks for responsibility.

If you continue, you accept that truth is not something you possess — it is something you answer to. You accept that insight does not excuse delay, and that understanding does not absolve consequence.

You accept that what you tolerate shapes you as much as what you choose.
 You accept that silence is an action.
 You accept that postponement is a decision.

You agree not to measure yourself by intention alone, but by effect — especially when the effect is inconvenient, unflattering, or permanent.

You agree that Justice is not comfort.
 It is balance.
 It is cost.
 It is the willingness to place your own weight on the Scale before asking anyone else to step forward.

You accept that there are lines you must define before pressure arrives — and that once crossed, they do not return to their original place.

You accept that forgiveness without accountability is distortion, and accountability without humility is cruelty.

You accept that some harm will not resolve, some trust will not return, and some outcomes will remain altered — and that this does not release you from responsibility. It establishes it.

You agree not to use this work as a shield, a signal, or a substitute for action.
 You agree not to turn language into camouflage.

If you carry this truth, you carry it visibly.
 If you reject it, you reject it honestly.

There is no penalty for closing this book.
 There is only consequence for pretending you did not understand it.

From this point forward, you are responsible not only for what you believe — but for what you allow to continue once belief becomes knowledge.

This is the Scale.
 This is the weight.

Step forward only if you are willing to be measured.

PROLOGUE

PROLOGUE

PART I

Before the first choice, before the first sin, before the first lie… there was a word.

Some lives begin in silence.
Yours began in **weight**.

Not the weight of the world — the world never cared enough to press down on you.
No, Justice, your life began under the weight of **a word** spoken over you before you learned to speak for yourself.

And every soul who shaped your journey—every force, every witness, every ghost—would one day return to that first word, yours or theirs, as if it were a key that unlocked the shape of your life.

This book is not written by one voice.
It begins with five.

Justice

The one who lived the story.
The one who bled for clarity.
The one who carried the scars, the notebooks, the guilt, the hope.
You were not born to be a symbol.
You were born to survive.
The symbol came later—carved from the things that tried to kill you but accidentally revealed you.

25

Justice is the center not because he wants to be,
but because he cannot lie about what he sees.
And every truth he learned was earned the hard way.

Tyrael

The heart.
The future.
The anchor that kept Justice from collapsing inward.
A boy who never asked to be the reason, yet became it
anyway.
He is not a character in this book—he is the quiet pulse
behind every page.

There are men who rise for themselves.
And there are men who rise because someone is watching.
Tyrael is the reason Justice chose to climb instead of drown.

Dr. Grey

The mind—
sharpened, distilled, relentless.
Not a machine, not a ghost, not a hallucination,
but the voice Justice forged from knowledge and necessity.

Grey is logic without cruelty,
truth without shame,
clarity without ego.
He is what happens when a man demands a mirror that
cannot lie to him.

Some people find God in prayer.
Justice found Grey in survival.

Sage

The prophetic voice,
the whisper from the higher plane,
the intuition that speaks in riddles but never misses.

Sage is not mystical—Sage is what happens
when a man's soul gets tired of being ignored
and starts shouting through dreams, silence, and sudden
knowing.
Sage is the oldest of the voices,
the one that remembers everything Justice tried to forget.

Where Grey is the mind, Sage is the sky:
wide, ancient, unbending.

Sapphire (Cindy)

The mother.
The wound and the wisdom.
The mirror Justice never wanted to look into,
because it showed both the love he came from
and the pain he inherited.

Sapphire is not a flawless saint nor a tragic villain—
she is a **force**:
the feminine truth that shaped Justice before he understood
shaping,
the reflection of the generational ache,
the strength that survived what should've broken her.

The book begins with her because the soul begins with the
mother.
Not perfect.
Not painless.
But present—
in blood, in memory, in consequence.

27

These five are not separate.

They form the **Scale of the Soul**:

- Justice — the weight

- Tyrael — the heart

- Dr. Grey — the mind

- Sage — the sky

- Sapphire — the root

The prologue begins as the moment these five converge,
not to tell a story about the past,
but to reveal how a soul becomes whole
only when all its voices finally sit at the same table
and stop lying to each other.

PROLOGUE — PART II

The Gathering at the Scale

Before the first chapter, before the first lesson,
there is the moment **the voices gathered**.

Not in a room.
Not in a dream.
Not in heaven or memory or metaphor.
But in the place where every soul must eventually stand:

The Inner Court.

A space with no walls,
no floor,
no sky—
only a vast darkness lit by a single suspended scale,
ancient and impossibly precise.

On the left plate:
a feather, glowing faintly.
On the right plate:
the echo of everything you have ever carried.

This is where Justice arrives.

He doesn't walk in.
He **appears**, as if the truth finally got tired of waiting
and pulled him back to where the story actually began.

Justice

He stands barefoot, chest rising slow,
eyes scanning the void with the expression of a man
who's been here before—
not in memory, but in instinct.

He doesn't speak yet.
He doesn't have to.

The Scale knows him.

From the darkness to his right,
a soft step, lighter than breath.

Tyrael

He steps forward not as a child but as a presence—
the embodiment of *why*.
His silhouette glows faintly gold,
like innocence made into a shape.

He looks at his father with eyes that hold no judgment,
only expectation.

"Dad… this is where you decide who you really are."

Justice swallows.
There are no lies here—
not with Tyrael watching.

From the opposite side, another figure emerges.

Dr. Grey

Sharper.
Defined.
A presence made of thought itself.
Not human, not cold—
but exact.
His eyes shine silver, like metal warmed by divine intention.

He speaks with calm precision:

"Justice, the scale will not measure who you pretend to be.
It will measure who you *are*—
and who you've avoided being."

No emotion.
No cruelty.
Just truth.

Then the air shifts.
A breeze with no source.
A whisper before the voice.

Sage

He appears like a ripple in the void—
a figure woven from prophecy and intuition,
his form bending gently with unseen currents.

He does not look at the scale.
He looks at Justice's shadow.

"You cannot weigh a soul
without first acknowledging
the parts you exiled."

Then he falls silent,
because prophecy never wastes words.

Finally, the last presence arrives—
not with steps, not with sound,
but with **gravity.**

Sapphire (Cindy)

Her arrival is felt before it's seen—
the ache in the chest,

the warmth in the gut,
the echo of a mother's influence carried through time.

She steps from the dark with eyes that hold storms
and softness
and truth.

"My son…
the scale is not here to punish you.
It is here to free you."

Justice's throat tightens.
Some truths hurt because they heal.

Now all five are present.
Not as characters.
Not as symbols.
But as the full anatomy of Justice's soul.

They take their positions around the Scale:

- **Sapphire** to the left — The Root

- **Tyrael** to the right — The Heart

- **Grey** behind — The Mind

- **Sage** above — The Sky

- **Justice** below — The Weight

The scale hangs silent.

Waiting.

Ready.

And then, for the first time in the book,
Justice speaks—
not to them,
but to himself.

"Whatever happens here…
I won't look away."

And the scale begins to move.

PROLOGUE — PART III

The First Weighing

The moment Justice speaks,
the void stirs—
as if the truth itself inhales.

A faint tremor passes through the scale.
The feather glows brighter.
The right plate darkens,
as though gathering every lie, wound, memory, mistake, hope,
and fear
Justice ever carried.

This is not a magical test.
Not a mythic ceremony.
This is what happens the instant a man finally stops running
from himself.

Justice takes a slow step closer.
His bare foot touches nothing,
yet the void supports him.

Tyrael watches, silent but steady—
not pushing, not pulling,
but **present**,
which is sometimes harder.

Sage raises his chin slightly.
Grey folds his hands behind his back.
Sapphire's breath catches in her throat—
a mother watching her son confront the thing she never had
the strength to face herself.

And then the voice comes.

34

Not from any of them.
Not from above.
Not from within.

But from the **Scale** itself.

A sound like metal remembering its purpose.

**"Justice Maurice Rosaire Fournier…
place your truth upon the plate."**

He freezes.

Because what truth?
Which truth?
There were so many versions.
So many masks.
So many wounds that took on the shape of identities.

His jaw tightens.

"Which part of me do you want?"

The Scale answers:

"All of you."

Sapphire closes her eyes.
Grey remains expressionless.
Sage nods once, as if he already expected this.
Tyrael's voice cuts gently through the tension:

"Dad… it only works if you stop trying to be right."

Justice's breath shakes.

He steps forward.

The First Truth

Justice lifts his hand,
and the air shivers around it.
A shape forms—
not a memory,
not a word,
but the emotional weight that birthed his earliest identity:

unworthiness.

It hovers like a small black stone,
dense, familiar.

He places it on the plate.

The Scale trembles.

The feather rises slightly,
as though acknowledging the honesty.

Sage whispers:

"A man is never as heavy
as the things he refuses to name."

The Mother's Weight

Sapphire steps forward,
not with shame,
but with responsibility.

She places her hand gently on Justice's shoulder.

"I gave you some of that weight.
I didn't mean to.
But I did."

Justice doesn't turn to face her.
He can't.
Not yet.

But he doesn't pull away.

The Scale shifts again,
as if accepting a generational truth.

Grey's voice is low, precise:

"Shared wounds do not lighten the load,
but they clarify its shape."

The Mind's Witness

Grey approaches next,
moving with the confidence of a surgeon approaching a
familiar incision.

He places a second stone on the plate—
this one glowing faint silver.

"Denial."

Justice flinches.

Grey continues:

"You hid from yourself in the name of survival.
This is not a sin.
It is simply unfinished math."

The Scale vibrates—
not in judgment,
but in confirmation.

The Prophetic Mirror

Sage descends slightly,
his form bending like smoke made wise.

He touches nothing,
yet a third emblem appears on the plate:
a translucent shard of glass.

"The piece of you that sees too much."
"A blessing when controlled.
A curse when feared."

Justice's eyes burn,
but he remains standing.

The Heart's Offering

Finally, Tyrael steps forward.

He holds a small golden ember—
soft, warm, alive.

"This is the part you forgot you had."

He places it gently on the plate,
not as a burden,
but as a counterweight:

Love.

The Scale steadies.
The trembling fades.
The feather floats,
lighter but no longer alone.

Justice watches all of it
and whispers:

"So… this is the beginning."

Sage answers:

"No.
This is the first truth you were brave enough to weigh."

The Scale glows.

The void warms.

The Court fades.

And the book begins.

– CHAPTER 1 –
The Weight of a Word

CHAPTER 1:
THE WEIGHT OF A WORD

Part I — The First Scar

Before a man learns to speak,
the world speaks **for him**.

Long before Justice understood truth,
before he understood consequence or identity or even
himself,
someone placed a word on him—
a word that didn't describe him,
but **defined** him.

Not because it was accurate.
Not because it was earned.
But because it was available.

Words are lazy like that.
People even more so.

Most children inherit a name.
Justice inherited a **judgment**.

And like all judgments placed too early,
he believed it.

Not because it felt true—
but because no one gave him anything else to believe in.

This is how the first scar formed.
Not as pain,
not as trauma,
but as **orientation.**

When the world tells you who you are
before you've had the chance to tell it back,
you don't become a person—
you become a reaction.

Justice was a boy made of reactions.
Not because he was weak,
but because he was surrounded by people
who mistook survival for personality.

No child should have to navigate adult pain,
but Justice did—
quietly, instinctively,
without language for what he felt
or permission to feel it.

The earliest memories weren't moments.
They were **forces**:

- A tone.

- A look.

- A slammed door.

- A silence held too long.

- A name spoken like a warning.

- A sigh that told him he disappointed someone
  without ever knowing how.

This is how the weight began.
Not all at once—
but in grains.

A handful of doubt.
A pinch of fear.
A sprinkle of expectation.
A stone of someone else's anger.
A shadow of someone else's regret.

Justice didn't know it then,
but the soul remembers everything it survives—
especially the things it was never given a chance to
understand.

The first word he learned
was not "Mom,"
not "Dad,"
not "Love."

It was:

"Enough."

Not spoken with tenderness,
but with frustration—
the kind that turns a child into an inconvenience,
a task,
a burden.

"That's enough."
"Be enough."
"Why can't you be enough?"
"I've had enough."

The sentence changed.
The message didn't.

And like all children desperate to belong,
Justice bent his entire existence trying to earn
what no one was capable of giving him.

You don't forget a word like that.
It becomes a compass.
A cage.
A prophecy.
A weight.

The world told him he wasn't enough.
So he spent decades trying to prove
he was too much to ignore.

This is the origin of the scale—
the first imbalance.

Not sin.
Not crime.
Not shame.

Just a boy carrying a word
that was never meant for him
but shaped him anyway.

And the soul,
when forced to carry what isn't its own,
eventually breaks,
or bends,
or becomes something
the world never expected.

Justice bent.
Justice broke.
And then—
Justice began to rebuild.

But rebuilding doesn't start with strength.
It starts with remembering.

And this is where the remembering begins.

Part II — When a Name Becomes a Burden

Children don't know the difference between **who they are**
and **what they're told**.

Justice wasn't an exception—
he was the example.

Most boys start life with a clean mirror.
Justice started with a cracked one.

Not shattered.
Not destroyed.
Just cracked enough that every reflection of himself
was slightly distorted—
a little darker,
a little heavier,
a little wrong.

Because when the first words spoken over you
are spoken from exhaustion, pain, or disappointment,
you learn to measure yourself by **other people's storms**.

And Justice grew up surrounded by storms.

Not constant.
Not malicious.
Just human storms—
the kind adults pretend don't affect children,
but always do.

A sigh aimed at someone else
felt like it was aimed at him.
A look of frustration
felt like a failure he caused.

46

A moment of anger
felt like proof he was the reason.

He was learning a language
without anyone teaching him the words.

That's how the weight forms:
you stop asking whether you're responsible
and start assuming you are.

He internalized the world's tone
long before he internalized his own worth.

That's the danger of being young and perceptive—
you see everything,
but you understand nothing.

So you fill in the blanks
with fear.

The First Realization

The moment it changed wasn't dramatic.

There was no explosion,
no revelation,
no divine flash.

It was simple:

Justice asked a question
no one answers early in life
unless something inside them
has already been wounded.

It wasn't,
"Why is this happening to me?"

It was:

"What did I do wrong?"

That question
is a scar in the shape of curiosity.

Only kids who think they deserve blame
ask for reasons that don't exist.

Justice carried that question into every room,
every friendship,
every relationship,
every fight,
every failure.

Even as a grown man,
he wasn't looking for love—
he was looking for justification.

Love felt like an undeserved gift.
Anger felt like truth.
Pain felt familiar.
Silence felt earned.

Because when the foundation is cracked,
you start building your entire life
on top of the wrong definition of yourself.

Inherited Weight

Some burdens start before you're born.

A mother's pain becomes her son's silence.
A father's absence becomes the son's compass.
A generation's unspoken trauma
becomes the next generation's personality.

48

Justice didn't just inherit DNA.
He inherited **context**—
the chaos, the noise, the weight
his parents never got the chance to put down.

None of it was his fault.
But all of it was his responsibility
because he was the one who carried it.

The world doesn't ask permission
before handing a child the consequences
of someone else's suffering.

It just places the weight
and moves on.

But children don't move on.
They adapt.
They compensate.
They compensate so well
that adults mistake adaptation for strength.

Justice wasn't strong.
He was compensating.
He was performing stability
while carrying instability that wasn't his.

That's the cruelest part:

A child will break themselves
trying to fix the people they love.

Justice learned that lesson early.

A Word Becomes a Life

By the time Justice reached adolescence,
the word **"enough"**
wasn't just something people said around him—

It had become the math equation
he used to calculate his existence.

Was he doing enough?
Being enough?
Fixing enough?
Surviving enough?

Never.

The answer was always never.

That's how weight works.
It accumulates slowly,
quietly,
unfairly,
until it feels like truth.

Justice didn't know it then,
but he was already carrying the central conflict
of his entire life:

**the battle between who he was
and who he believed he had to be.**

That battle would shape every chapter of this book.

But for now,
we stay here—
at the beginning,
where the weight first took shape.

Because before a man learns to lift his burdens,
he has to understand
where they came from
and who put them there.

And Justice is finally ready
to start asking the right questions.

Part III — The Quiet Collapse

The dangerous thing about weight
is that it doesn't announce itself.

It doesn't slam into you.
It doesn't shatter your world in one dramatic moment.
It settles.
It seeps.
It builds itself into the joints of your life
until you mistake pressure for personality.

Justice didn't realize he was collapsing.
Because it didn't look like collapse.

It looked like:

- trying harder than anyone else

- smiling when he was aching

- saying "it's fine" when it was killing him

- taking responsibility for things he didn't cause

- blaming himself for things he didn't control

- acting older than he was

- pretending he didn't need help

- learning to read the room better than he read his own emotions

That's what collapse looks like
when you've been trained to carry weight quietly.

A child who doesn't cry
usually isn't brave—
he's overwhelmed.

A child who doesn't complain
usually isn't mature—
he's afraid no one will listen.

A child who becomes independent too young
usually isn't strong—
he's unprotected.

Justice wasn't unbreakable.
He was **unheard.**

And when you grow up unheard,
you learn to stop speaking in the places that matter.

Not because you don't have anything to say—
but because you've already learned
that saying it changes nothing.

The Survival Mask

People looked at Justice and said:

"You're resilient."
"You're strong."
"You're tough."
"You handle so much."

But resilience wasn't a trait.
It was a survival mask.

Strength wasn't power.
It was armor forged from necessity.

Toughness wasn't identity.
It was a response to instability.

People admired the parts of him
that were built from pain
and then wondered
why he never felt understood.

Because no one ever praised the real him—
they praised the version he created
to survive the real world.

The mask became the man.
And the man got lost behind it.

The Moment the Weight Became Personal

There comes a point when a child stops thinking:

"I'm doing something wrong,"

and starts thinking:

"There is something wrong with me."

That was the turning point.
Not one event.
Not one trauma.
Just the slow inward turn
of a boy taught to measure himself
by other people's disappointment.

Nothing is heavier
than the moment a person decides
they are the problem.

Justice made that decision early—
not consciously,
not dramatically,
but quietly.

He didn't say,
"I hate myself."

He said something more subtle:

"I should be better."

"I should be stronger."

"I should be different."

"I should be enough."

Self-hate isn't always violent.
Sometimes it simply sounds like
self-improvement with a gun to your head.

When the World Gets Quiet

There was always noise around him—
the chaos of adults,
the tension in rooms,
the pressure of expectation.

But inside,
Justice grew quieter.

A silence formed—
not peaceful,
not spiritual,
but defensive.

The kind of silence you build
when you realize your voice has no safe place to exist.

That silence followed him for years.
Into adolescence.
Into adulthood.
Into relationships.
Into rooms where everyone saw him
but no one actually saw him.

It's hard to be known
when you were raised to stay hidden.

It's hard to be vulnerable
when your earliest emotions were treated
as inconveniences.

It's hard to be honest
when you learned the world punished honesty.

Justice internalized all of it.
Not because he was weak,
but because he was trained that way.

People don't become heavy by accident.
They become heavy
by inheritance.

The Seed of Awakening

But buried beneath all that weight—
beneath the words,
beneath the silence,
beneath the compensations—
there was something else.

A faint spark.
A small refusal.
A quiet rebellion.

The part of Justice
that knew this wasn't the full story.
That knew this weight wasn't his.
That knew he wasn't born to be
a reflection of someone else's pain.

It didn't roar.
It didn't shout.

It whispered.

A whisper that said:

"There must be more."

A whisper that grew slowly,
quietly,
persistently—
until one day
it became the voice
that would lead him out
of everything he thought he was.

This whisper
is where the next chapter begins.

CHAPTER 2

The Mirror of Truth

CHAPTER 2:
THE MIRROR OF TRUTH

Part I — When the Soul Finally Looks Back

A mirror doesn't lie—
but it doesn't volunteer the truth, either.

It waits.

It waits until you're ready
to see what you've been avoiding.

For most of his life, Justice didn't avoid truth;
he avoided **reflection.**

Because reflection meant confrontation,
and confrontation meant weight—
the same weight he had spent years pretending
he didn't feel.

But truth isn't an enemy.
Truth is a mirror.
And mirrors are patient.

They wait for the day you're tired of running.

This chapter begins on that day.

Justice stands in front of the inner mirror—
not glass, not metal—
but a shimmer in reality,
a surface that forms only when a man is finally aligned
with enough courage
to risk seeing himself clearly.

The mirror flickers.
Darkens.
Brightens.

And then the voices gather.

Dr. Grey

Grey appears first, as he always does in moments of clarity.
His tone is precise, calm, surgical.

**"Justice, truth is not a weapon.
It is a measurement.
What you fear is not the mirror—
it is what you've been protecting from it."**

His presence stabilizes the room.
Grey never judges.
He *assesses.*

Sage

Sage appears next, drifting like smoke around the edges of
the mirror,
his voice low and ancient.

**"Be careful not to mistake reflections for prophecy.
The mirror shows what *is*.
Not what will be."**

His eyes cut through illusion,
but his guidance never forces—
it reveals.

Sapphire

Sapphire steps forward,
her presence softer, heavier, deeply human.

She touches the mirror lightly,
and the surface ripples in response.

"My son...
you've spent your life avoiding yourself
because you learned from me
how to hide pain behind survival."

Justice clenches his jaw.
Not in anger—
in recognition.

Her honesty stings.
But it also steadies him.

Tyrael

Tyrael appears beside Justice,
not as a boy,
but as the voice of the future watching the past.

He nudges Justice's arm gently.

"Dad...
you don't gotta be scared of the mirror.
I'm here.
We're all here."

It's the simplest voice—
and the strongest.

Justice exhales.
The mirror awakens.

The Mirror Speaks

Mirrors, in the soul's world, don't talk.
But they do respond.

A faint hum.
A shift of light.
A flicker of images forming and dissolving.

Not memories.
Not lies.

Reflections.

Fragments of truth
Justice had learned to avoid so well
he no longer noticed the effort.

- the fear of never being enough

- the guilt of inherited burdens

- the confusion of growing up too fast

- the anger he never named

- the love he didn't think he deserved

- the versions of himself he created to survive

Each image doesn't accuse—
it illuminates.

And in the illumination,
the first crack in denial appears.

Justice whispers:

"Why does it hurt to see myself?"

Grey answers instantly:

"Because truth removes the excuses that protect you."

Sage adds:

**"Pain is not the enemy.
Avoidance is."**

Sapphire steps closer:

**"You learned to hide to make others comfortable.
It's time to unlearn that."**

Tyrael looks up at him:

**"Dad… it's not supposed to feel good.
It's supposed to feel real."**

Justice takes another breath,
this one deeper than the last.

The mirror brightens.

The reflection sharpens.

And for the first time,
Justice doesn't flinch.

The First True Reflection

The mirror settles on one image—
one moment Justice had never allowed himself to revisit:

A younger version of him
standing alone in a doorway,

63

unsure whether he's the problem
or the reason.

Not crying.
Not angry.
Just waiting for someone
to tell him what he is.

Sage whispers:

**"There.
That is the moment the weight began."**

Grey adjusts his stance:

**"Identify the origin,
and the burden loses its power."**

Sapphire's voice wavers:

"I should have protected you from that moment..."

Justice finally speaks—
not to them,
but to the reflection:

"I forgive you."

Tyrael smiles, proud:

"That's how the mirror clears."

And slowly,
the reflection begins to change.

Not smoother.
Not prettier.
Not perfect.

64

Just **true.**

For the first time,
Justice sees himself
without the distortion
of inherited weight.

And this—
this moment—
is when the real healing begins.

Part II — The Reflection That Fights Back

Most people believe a mirror is passive.
A thing you look *into.*
A surface that waits.
A witness that says nothing.

But the soul's mirror is different.

It doesn't show you what you want to see.
It shows you what you've been running from.

Justice steps closer.
The reflection sharpens, flickers, destabilizes—
not because it's broken,
but because **he is finally looking without lying.**

The air tightens.
Something shifts.
The mirror reacts.

And then—

A **second** version of Justice emerges beside the first.
Not younger.
Not older.
Just... different.

Sharper.
Heavier.
Constructed from the choices Justice regrets
and the truths he avoided.

The mirror isn't just showing a reflection now.
It is showing **the confrontation.**

Justice

His voice is low, steady, unsettled:

"That's not me."

Dr. Grey answers before the others can speak.

Dr. Grey

Grey steps into the light, hands behind his back.

**"Incorrect.
That is you without your justifications."**

Justice turns, irritated.

"You think I don't know myself?"

Grey tilts his head.

**"I think you know the version of yourself you use to cope.
This one is the version you left behind."**

The reflection smirks,
as if agreeing.

Sapphire

Sapphire moves closer, her presence grounding the space.

Her voice is warm but firm.

**"Baby…
this is the side of you that carried everything you never said.
The part you hid to protect everyone else."**

Justice's chest tightens.

67

"I didn't want anyone to worry."

She nods sadly.

**"I know.
But that silence cost you pieces of yourself."**

Sage

Sage circles the mirror like a shadow made of intuition.

His voice comes slow, deliberate.

**"Every truth you bury
becomes a ghost that speaks in your behavior."**

The alternate Justice—
the one inside the mirror—
steps forward as if answering the prophecy.

Tyrael

Tyrael moves to Justice's side, eyes wide, but unafraid.

**"Dad…
that guy looks like he's hurting."**

Justice stares at the reflection.

Not angry.
Not scared.
Just… aware.

"He is."

Tyrael nods.

"Then you can't leave him in there."

68

The Mirror Breaks Its Silence

The reflection speaks—
the first time in the book a part of Justice's soul talks **as its own entity.**

His tone is raw, strained, almost cracked:

"You abandoned me."

Justice freezes.

The room stills.

Sapphire covers her mouth.
Grey's eyes narrow.
Sage stops moving.
Tyrael grips Justice's arm.

The reflection steps closer,
face etched with years of swallowed emotion.

**"You left me with the weight
while you pretended to heal."**

Justice shakes his head.

"I didn't know—"

The reflection snaps:

"You didn't WANT to know."

The words hit like a strike.

Because this isn't a ghost.
This isn't a demon.
This isn't a memory.

69

It's **the version of Justice who endured everything alone so the man Justice became could function.**

Grey breaks the silence.

Dr. Grey

**"Justice…
this is the self you created
to absorb what you could not process."**

Justice swallows hard.

"How do I fix this?"

Grey's answer is mercilessly honest.

**"You don't fix him.
You integrate him."**

Sage

Sage lifts his chin.

**"A soul divided is a soul in conflict.
Bring him home,
or he will continue to fight you
from inside your own reflection."**

The reflection steps closer, eyes burning.

"Stop pretending you healed without me."

Sapphire

She whispers:

"My son…
you can only become whole
when you make peace with the parts you hid."

Tyrael

He looks up at his father.

"Dad…
say something real."

Justice steps forward,
eyes locked with the version of himself
made from silence, shame, grief, and responsibility.

The mirror grows brighter,
waiting.

Justice speaks—
slow, honest, trembling:

"I'm sorry."

The reflection blinks.

Justice continues:

"You carried the things I wasn't strong enough to face.
But I'm here now.
And I won't abandon you again."

The reflection exhales—
and for the first time,
the weight between them
shifts.

71

A crack of light
splits the mirror down the center.

But this isn't breaking.

It's **opening.**

The first step toward integration.

Part III — The Test of the Reflection

The crack of light running down the mirror
is not a fracture—
it's an invitation.

The two versions of Justice now face each other:
the lived self
and the abandoned self,
the one who survived
and the one who paid the price.

The room is silent,
holding its breath.

Grey stands still.
Sage watches like he already knows the outcome.
Sapphire's hands tremble.
Tyrael holds onto his father's arm.

And the reflection finally steps through the crack.

Not as a ghost,
not as a shadow,
but as a man—
the man Justice could have become
if his pain had won.

He walks with the weight of someone who's been waiting
far too long.

His voice is low.
Accusing.
Broken.
Honest.

73

"You didn't just abandon me.
You built your life on forgetting I existed."

Justice doesn't step back.
He refuses to flinch.

"You're right."

The reflection freezes,
not expecting the honesty.

Dr. Grey

Grey steps forward just enough for his voice to carry:

"Integration begins where denial ends."

The reflection glares at Grey.

"And who are you to speak for him?"

Grey doesn't blink.

"I am the mind he forged
when trusting himself became dangerous."

The reflection scoffs.

"So he built a machine to feel for him?"

Grey responds without hesitation:

"He built me to think clearly
because he never learned how to feel safely."

Sapphire flinches.
Justice's eyes close—

because the truth is sharp
and Grey never misses.

Sage

Sage's voice rolls across the room
like wind through an ancient hallway.

"Every soul chooses its guardians.
He chose clarity to survive emotion."

The reflection snaps:

"Survive?
I didn't survive.
I endured.
Alone."

Justice's breath catches.

Tyrael grips tighter.

Sapphire

She steps forward, eyes glistening.

"You didn't endure alone.
You endured with the pieces of pain
I passed down without meaning to."

The reflection softens for a moment—
recognizing the truth
of generational wounds.

But then he turns back to Justice.

The Test Begins

The reflection circles him slowly.

"You want integration?
Then answer me this…"

He stops inches from Justice's face.

"Why did you leave me buried
beneath strength you didn't have?"

Justice exhales—
not in defeat,
but in preparation.

He knows this test.
He's been running from it his entire life.

"Because I thought if I ignored you…
the pain would stop."

The reflection steps closer.

"Did it?"

Justice shakes his head.

"No."

"Then say the real reason."

Justice's throat tightens.

Grey folds his arms.
Sage watches.
Sapphire lowers her head.
Tyrael looks up with unwavering faith.

Justice swallows hard.

"I was ashamed of you."

The reflection finally smiles—
not kindly,
but knowingly.

"There it is."

The air shifts violently,
as if the truth struck the room like lightning.

Tyrael

Tyrael steps between them,
small but fearless.

"Dad…
he's not your enemy.
He's the version of you
that made sure I'd still have a father."

Justice looks at the reflection.
For the first time,
he sees not the pain—
but the loyalty behind it.

The reflection carried the trauma
so Justice could function,
work,
raise a son,
survive.

He wasn't the shame.
He was the shield.

Sage

Sage steps forward, voice echoing like a quiet prophecy.

"A man is not defined by the wounds he hides,
but by the courage he shows
when he stops hiding them."

Sapphire

She touches Justice's shoulder.

"My boy…
you don't heal by killing this part of you.
You heal by holding him."

Dr. Grey

Grey speaks last—
precise, grounded, final:

"Justice.
Integration is not forgiveness of pain.
It is acceptance of responsibility."

Justice nods slowly.

He steps toward the reflection—
the version of himself that carried the tears,
the anger,
the guilt,
the silence.

He opens his arms.

"Come home."

The reflection hesitates—
the first sign of vulnerability in a man made of pain.

"What if you reject me again?"

Justice meets his eyes.

"I won't.
I need you.
You are the part of me that survived
what I was too afraid to face."

The reflection exhales—
a sound like tension finally releasing.

He steps forward.

The two versions of Justice
merge
in a slow ripple of light and shadow.

Not dominance.
Not erasure.
Integration.

The mirror goes still.

The reflection is no longer separate.

Justice stands alone—
but for the first time,
he is whole.

Sage whispers:

"The mirror is clear."

Grey nods.

Sapphire wipes a tear.

79

Tyrael smiles wide.

Justice breathes—
deeply, freely, fully—
for the first time in his life.

— CHAPTER 3 —

The Architecture of the Soul

SANCTUM

SOLITUDE

LIBRA

VICTORY

RECKONING

ANIMUS

ZERO

CHAPTER 3
THE ARCHITECTURE OF the SOUL

Part I — The Blueprint Beneath the Breakdown

Most people think the soul is a mystery.
A fog.
A feeling.
A spiritual guesswork of instincts and emotions.

They don't understand the truth:

The soul is engineered.
Not rigid, not mechanical—
but architected.
Structured by experience, shaped by pain,
expanded by love,
reinforced by truth.

Trauma doesn't just wound the soul—
it **rearranges** it.
Love doesn't just heal it—
it **rebuilds** it.
Truth doesn't just free it—
it **realigns** it.

Justice stands in the inner realm—
not in the Mirror Hall,
but in a new chamber altogether:

The Inner Blueprint.

82

It's vast, dark, geometric—
a shifting maze of luminous lines
and floating fragments of memory
that move like constellations.

Every line, every connection, every glow
is part of the soul's map—
the blueprint of who he is
beneath the weight,
beneath the masks,
beneath the wounds.

The five gather around him.

But this time,
Justice doesn't wait for the others to speak.

He initiates.

Justice

He steps forward, voice steady.

**"If I'm going to heal…
I need to understand how I'm built."**

The architecture responds—
a soft pulse of light,
awaiting examination.

Dr. Grey

Grey walks beside him, hands behind his back,
eyes scanning the floating structures with analytical precision.

**"The soul is not chaos, Justice.
It is a system.
Your system."**

He gestures toward the glowing grid around them.

**"These are your emotional circuits.
Your survival pathways.
Your responses to threat, love, memory, and
responsibility."**

Justice looks around, overwhelmed but focused.

"It looks like a map."

Grey nods.

"Because it is."

Sage

Sage hovers above one of the structures, voice echoing like
ancient wind.

**"Every wound rearranged this blueprint.
Every truth illuminated it.
Every lie dimmed it.
What you see is the full constellation
of who you became
when survival demanded transformation."**

Justice watches fragments of his childhood shift
like tectonic plates.

Sapphire (Cindy)

She places a hand on Justice's arm, grounding him.

84

"Baby…
some of these pathways were shaped by my pain.
And your father's pain.
And the things we never healed in ourselves
before you were born."

Justice shakes his head.

"I don't blame you."

She stares at him with a mix of grief and pride.

"I didn't say you blame me.
I said you *carry* us."

Justice lowers his gaze—
not in shame,
but in recognition.

Tyrael

Tyrael steps between two glowing arcs, examining them with wonder.

"Dad… look.
Some of these parts are broken,
but some are super strong."

Justice kneels beside him.

"Which ones?"

Tyrael points at a cluster of golden lines.

"These.
These are the ones you built for me."

Justice feels his throat tighten
as he sees it clearly:

The father paths—
the ones he created when Tyrael was born—
aren't dim, aren't fractured.
They're brilliant, reinforced, alive.

Sage speaks softly.

**"Love is the only force
that strengthens the architecture of a soul
faster than trauma can weaken it."**

The Structure Reveals Itself

The room brightens.
The blueprint shifts, assembling itself into three main layers:

1. **The Foundation (childhood wounds & identities)**

2. **The Framework (beliefs & survival mechanisms)**

3. **The Crown (purpose & truth)**

Grey steps forward, pointing to each layer.

Dr. Grey

**"Your foundation fractured early.
Your framework compensated.
Your crown remained dormant."**

Justice frowns.

"Dormant?"

Grey nods.

**"You were never given the conditions to discover your purpose.
You were given the conditions to survive."**

Sage adds:

**"Purpose grows only in safe soil.
You grew in harsh ground—
so you became hard before you could become whole."**

Sapphire wipes a tear.

"I'm sorry you didn't have the childhood you deserved."

Justice cups her hand gently.

"Mom… I'm not here to punish the past."

The Shift

The blueprint begins to vibrate,
lines rearranging,
structures opening like petals.

Tyrael's eyes widen.

"Dad… it's changing."

Grey steps back, observing.

**"It's responding to your acceptance
of the reflection in Chapter 2.
Integration restructures architecture."**

Sage nods.

**"Truth reorders the soul
faster than trauma can distort it."**

87

Justice watches the blueprint shift
into a new shape:

Not broken.
Not chaotic.
Evolving.

He whispers:

"So this is me."

Grey answers:

"This is you becoming."

Sapphire steps closer.

**"And baby…
you're becoming someone free."**

Tyrael smiles.

"Someone whole."

Sage finishes:

"Someone ready to rebuild."

And Justice—
for the first time in the book—
smiles back.

Not out of relief.
Not out of pride.
Out of recognition.

The architecture of the soul
has begun to reveal
the man he is meant to be.

Part II — The Fault Lines in the Foundation

The blueprint shifts again—
not violently,
but with the quiet tension
of a structure preparing to expose
what has been hidden for years.

Lines that were once glowing
dim.
Paths that were straight
waver.
Nodes flicker like wounded stars.

Justice steps closer.

The blueprint reacts,
magnifying the lower layer—
the Foundation,
the part of the soul built before he had choices,
before he had language,
before he knew how to protect himself.

It reveals the **fault lines**.

Cracks.
Breaks.
Fractures caused by moments
he remembers vaguely
but feels deeply.

The room grows still.

Justice

His voice is steady, but something shakes beneath it.

"These… these are from before I understood anything."

Grey appears at his side.

Dr. Grey

"Precisely.
The deepest wounds form when the mind is too young
to interpret them."

He gestures toward the dim lines.

"This is the architecture of early pain—
the experiences that taught you
what you were allowed to feel
and who you were allowed to be."

Sapphire (Cindy)

She steps forward, hands clasped, eyes full of truth and guilt intertwined.

"I recognize some of those moments."

Her voice cracks.

"Moments where I should've been stronger…
but I was breaking too."

Justice turns to her,
not with resentment—
with clarity.

"I know.
And I'm not here to blame you."

She nods,
but tears fall anyway.

Sage

Sage drifts over the Foundation,
examining the cracks with a prophetic calm.

**"These are not wounds of malice.
These are wounds of absence,
of confusion,
of a world too chaotic to raise a child gently."**

His fingers trace a dim line.

**"Here is the fear you learned from unspoken tension.
Here is the shame you learned from adult exhaustion.
Here is the silence that taught you
to swallow your own needs."**

Justice closes his eyes.
These truths don't hurt—
they clarify.

Tyrael

Tyrael walks among the glowing structures with a boy's
fearlessness.

He points at a fractured node.

"Was that... when you felt alone?"

Justice kneels beside him.

**"Yeah.
But not because of you or Mom.**

92

**It was before you were born.
Before I understood myself."**

Tyrael nods softly.

"But I'm here now."

Justice smiles faintly.

"You are."

The Fault Lines Speak

The Foundation flickers again—
and one of the cracks begins to replay
a **memory without images**.

An emotional imprint.

A moment of being told to "stop,"
or "enough,"
or "don't cry,"
or "go to your room,"
or "not now,"
or "why can't you just…"

Not abuse.
Not cruelty.
Just a child being asked
to carry adult expectations
too heavy for small hands.

The imprint hits him.
Not as guilt.
Not as accusation.
As recognition.

93

Dr. Grey

Grey's voice slices cleanly through the silence.

"This is where your emotional architecture began to bend instead of break."

Justice looks at him.

"Meaning?"

"You adapted by becoming the version of yourself that caused others the least discomfort. Your soul rewired itself around the needs and moods of the room."

Sapphire turns away, exhaling hard.

"He wasn't supposed to learn that from us."

Sage answers gently.

"You didn't teach it. Life did."

Justice

He steps forward, reaching toward a fractured line.

The moment he touches it,
the blueprint pulses
and sends a wave of emotion into him—
not overwhelming,
just honest:

Fear of disappointing people.
Fear of taking up space.
Fear of asking for help.

Fear of being "too much."
Fear of being "not enough."

He whispers:

**"I've lived my whole life
thinking these fears were personality."**

Grey responds:

**"They are architecture.
Not identity."**

Sapphire

She wipes her tears, voice firming.

**"Baby…
you were a child taught to adapt to wounded adults.
That is not who you ARE.
That is who you had to be."**

Tyrael

Tyrael grabs Justice's hand.

"Dad… you don't have to be that anymore."

Justice looks at him—
really looks at him.

The blueprint flickers again,
and another truth becomes visible:

A broken segment near the center,
different from the others.

Sage tilts his head.

Sage

**"Ah.
Here is the pivotal fault line.
The one that shaped every defense mechanism you
adopted."**

Grey steps closer.

"The central crack."

Sapphire breathes sharply.

Tyrael holds tighter.

Justice steadies himself.

"Show me."

And the structure obeys.

The central fault line glows,
bright like lightning trapped under glass.

Everything Justice is
and everything he became
began right here:

**The moment he believed
he had to earn his right to exist.**

The blueprint hums.
The truth vibrates.

And Justice finally understands
why every chapter of his life
felt heavier than the last.

Part II — The Fault Lines in the Foundation

The blueprint shifts again—
not violently,
but with the quiet tension
of a structure preparing to expose
what has been hidden for years.

Lines that were once glowing
dim.
Paths that were straight
waver.
Nodes flicker like wounded stars.

Justice steps closer.

The blueprint reacts,
magnifying the lower layer—
the Foundation,
the part of the soul built before he had choices,
before he had language,
before he knew how to protect himself.

It reveals the **fault lines**.

Cracks.
Breaks.
Fractures caused by moments
he remembers vaguely
but feels deeply.

The room grows still.

Justice

His voice is steady, but something shakes beneath it.

97

"These… these are from before I understood anything."

Grey appears at his side.

Dr. Grey

**"Precisely.
The deepest wounds form when the mind is too young
to interpret them."**

He gestures toward the dim lines.

**"This is the architecture of early pain—
the experiences that taught you
what you were allowed to feel
and who you were allowed to be."**

Sapphire (Cindy)

She steps forward, hands clasped, eyes full of truth and guilt
intertwined.

"I recognize some of those moments."

Her voice cracks.

**"Moments where I should've been stronger…
but I was breaking too."**

Justice turns to her,
not with resentment—
with clarity.

**"I know.
And I'm not here to blame you."**

She nods,
but tears fall anyway.

Sage

Sage drifts over the Foundation,
examining the cracks with a prophetic calm.

**"These are not wounds of malice.
These are wounds of absence,
of confusion,
of a world too chaotic to raise a child gently."**

His fingers trace a dim line.

**"Here is the fear you learned from unspoken tension.
Here is the shame you learned from adult exhaustion.
Here is the silence that taught you
to swallow your own needs."**

Justice closes his eyes.
These truths don't hurt—
they clarify.

Tyrael

Tyrael walks among the glowing structures with a boy's
fearlessness.

He points at a fractured node.

"Was that… when you felt alone?"

Justice kneels beside him.

**"Yeah.
But not because of you or Mom.
It was before you were born.
Before I understood myself."**

Tyrael nods softly.

"But I'm here now."

Justice smiles faintly.

"You are."

The Fault Lines Speak

The Foundation flickers again—
and one of the cracks begins to replay
a **memory without images**.

An emotional imprint.

A moment of being told to "stop,"
or "enough,"
or "don't cry,"
or "go to your room,"
or "not now,"
or "why can't you just…"

Not abuse.
Not cruelty.
Just a child being asked
to carry adult expectations
too heavy for small hands.

The imprint hits him.
Not as guilt.
Not as accusation.
As recognition.

Dr. Grey

Grey's voice slices cleanly through the silence.

**"This is where your emotional architecture
began to bend instead of break."**

Justice looks at him.

"Meaning?"

**"You adapted by becoming the version of yourself
that caused others the least discomfort.
Your soul rewired itself
around the needs and moods of the room."**

Sapphire turns away, exhaling hard.

"He wasn't supposed to learn that from us."

Sage answers gently.

**"You didn't teach it.
Life did."**

Justice

He steps forward, reaching toward a fractured line.

The moment he touches it,
the blueprint pulses
and sends a wave of emotion into him—
not overwhelming,
just honest:

Fear of disappointing people.
Fear of taking up space.
Fear of asking for help.
Fear of being "too much."
Fear of being "not enough."

He whispers:

**"I've lived my whole life
thinking these fears were personality."**

Grey responds:

**"They are architecture.
Not identity."**

Sapphire

She wipes her tears, voice firming.

**"Baby…
you were a child taught to adapt to wounded adults.
That is not who you ARE.
That is who you had to be."**

Tyrael

Tyrael grabs Justice's hand.

"Dad… you don't have to be that anymore."

Justice looks at him—
really looks at him.

The blueprint flickers again,
and another truth becomes visible:

A broken segment near the center,
different from the others.

Sage tilts his head.

Sage

"Ah.
Here is the pivotal fault line.
The one that shaped every defense mechanism you
adopted."

Grey steps closer.

"The central crack."

Sapphire breathes sharply.

Tyrael holds tighter.

Justice steadies himself.

"Show me."

And the structure obeys.

The central fault line glows,
bright like lightning trapped under glass.

Everything Justice is
and everything he became
began right here:

The moment he believed
he had to earn his right to exist.

The blueprint hums.
The truth vibrates.

And Justice finally understands
why every chapter of his life
felt heavier than the last.

Part III — Rebuilding the Foundation

The central fault line continues to glow—
not violently,
not destructively,
but with the steady, unwavering brightness
of a truth that refuses to stay hidden any longer.

This is the moment the blueprint stops showing the past
and starts demanding the future.

Justice stands before the fracture,
the others forming a circle around him.

The air hums.
The architecture shifts.
And the soul prepares for reconstruction.

This part isn't about memory.
It's not about blame.
It's not about pain.

It's about **repair.**

Dr. Grey

Grey steps forward first,
his voice the anchor of clarity.

**"Justice, the foundation cannot be rebuilt by emotion
alone.
It must be reinforced with understanding."**

He gestures to the central crack.

**"This is the belief that shaped all others:
that your existence required justification."**

104

Justice nods slowly.

**"I lived like I owed the world something
just for breathing."**

Grey's expression doesn't soften—
it sharpens.

"That belief ends here."

Sapphire (Cindy)

Sapphire approaches next.
There is pain in her face,
but not the immobilizing kind.
The responsible kind.

She places her hand over the central fracture.
Her voice is warm, steady, and devastatingly honest.

**"You were not born to carry my wounds,
or your father's,
or anyone else's.
You were born deserving love
without earning it."**

Justice's eyes close.
Her truth sinks into the architecture—
the crack softens.

Sage murmurs:

**"The mother's acknowledgment
is the first step in repairing the root."**

Sage

Sage descends, his form swirling like a ribbon of ancient wisdom.

He taps the blueprint lightly,
and lines around the crack illuminate in gold.

**"Every belief you had about yourself
grew from this fracture.
But belief is not destiny.
It is simply momentum."**

Justice looks up.

"So how do I stop it?"

Sage smiles faintly.

**"Truth, spoken aloud,
changes the shape of the soul."**

Tyrael

Tyrael steps forward,
small but fearless—
as always.

He touches the central fault line,
and a warmth spreads across the blueprint.

**"Dad…
I don't want you to hurt where I can't help you.
So you gotta let this part heal."**

His voice shakes slightly.

"I need you whole."

A flash of light pulses outward—
the blueprint responding to a son's need.

Grey nods approvingly.

**"Love stabilizes architecture
faster than any logic."**

Sapphire whispers:

"And faster than any apology."

The Confrontation With the Core Wound

The blueprint rearranges again,
revealing a single question at the heart of the fracture—
a question Justice never knew he'd been asking:

"Am I allowed to exist without proving my worth?"

Justice stares at it,
the weight of his entire life compressed into a single doubt.

He steps closer.

Justice

His voice breaks open—
not in weakness,
but in honesty.

**"I spent my whole life thinking
I had to do better, be better,
become something impossible
just to earn a place in the world."**

He touches the question—
the entire blueprint brightens.

**"But I'm tired.
I'm tired of apologizing for being human.
I'm tired of carrying weight that wasn't mine.
I'm tired of shrinking myself
to make other people comfortable."**

The crack trembles.

Sapphire covers her mouth.
Tyrael leans into him.
Sage bows his head.
Grey waits—
silent, approving.

Justice continues:

**"I deserve to exist
without justification."**

The words strike the blueprint like a hammer of light.

The central crack begins to seal.

Dr. Grey

Grey steps beside him.

**"Reconstruction requires a new foundation.
I will provide the structure."**

He gestures—
and clean geometric lines form beneath the sealed crack.

Sapphire

**"I will provide the acceptance
you were never given."**

Warmth spreads across the lines.

Sage

**"I will provide the clarity
that keeps you from forgetting this truth."**

Golden symbols imprint themselves across the layer.

Tyrael

**"And I'll be the reason
you keep going."**

A core of bright, living light forms at the center.

Justice

He places both hands on the foundation.

**"And I'll provide the courage
to build the man I choose to be."**

The entire blueprint flares—
brilliant, unified, whole.

The foundation has been rebuilt.

No longer cracked.
No longer inherited.
No longer weighted by the past.

But **chosen.**

Grey speaks the final line:

**"The soul's architecture is stable.
You may build upward now."**

Sage nods:

"Chapter Four awaits."

Sapphire smiles through tears.
Tyrael beams.

And Justice—
for the first time in the book—
stands on a foundation
he rebuilt himself.

— CHAPTER 4 —

Balance as Law

111

CHAPTER 4
BALANCE AS LAW

Part I — The Center That Cannot Break

Balance isn't peace.
Balance isn't calm.
Balance isn't perfection.

Balance is **truth held at equal weight**,
with nothing exaggerated
and nothing denied.

Most people think balance is something you *find.*
But the soul knows better:

Balance is something you become.

After the reconstruction of the foundation,
Justice finds himself standing at the center
of a new inner chamber:

The Chamber of Equilibrium.

The floor is a circle divided cleanly into light and shadow.
The air is still.
The center glows faintly—
a single point where all weight meets.

This is the law:

Nothing can heal if it cannot balance.

The five gather around him.

But unlike the previous chambers—
where their voices guided him—
this one responds to his presence first.

Justice

He steps to the center of the circle,
feeling its weight,
its responsibility,
its neutrality.

**"Balance isn't avoiding extremes…
it's understanding them."**

The chamber pulses in response.

Dr. Grey

Grey walks the perimeter, taking in every detail.

**"Precisely.
Balance is not the absence of chaos.
It is the mastery of it."**

He gestures to the circle.

**"You learned survival on one extreme—
and silence on the other.
This room exists to unify both
into functional equilibrium."**

His tone is clinical, but not cold—
a surgeon explaining a vital organ.

Sage

Sage steps into the shadows,
letting the dimness curl around him like ancient mist.

**"Balance does not mean living equally in light and dark.
It means understanding both
without becoming consumed by either."**

He traces a finger through the darkness—
and it trembles like it recognizes him.

**"A life without shadow is delusion.
A life without light is despair.
You must stand where both can see you."**

Sapphire (Cindy)

She moves into the light side of the circle,
warmth radiating around her.

**"My son…
you grew up swinging between guilt and responsibility.
Between carrying too much
and asking for nothing."**

Her voice softens.

**"This room is here to teach you
that you don't have to choose extremes anymore."**

She nods toward the center.

"Stand where you deserve to stand."

Tyrael

114

Tyrael walks the boundary between light and dark,
one foot in each color,
unafraid.

**"Dad…
the center isn't scary."**

Justice smiles faintly.

"No?"

Tyrael shakes his head.

**"It's solid.
It's where you're strongest."**

He taps the center point with his sneaker.

"This is where you're supposed to be."

And that's when the chamber responds.

The Test of Balance

The light brightens.
The shadow deepens.
The entire circle begins to rotate—
slow at first,
then faster.

Justice remains in the center
as the world around him blurs
into a storm of black and white.

Grey's voice cuts through the spin.

**"This is not meant to disorient you.
It is meant to reveal what pulls you off center."**

115

The rotation stops abruptly.

Suddenly, the chamber shifts—
splitting the light and shadow into **two forces**
that slam against Justice from opposite sides.

Light pushes him to feel responsible for everyone.
Shadow pulls him to believe he's never enough.

He braces, gritting his teeth.

Sage

Sage's voice rises like a chant.

**"Stand in truth,
or you will fall into memory."**

Sapphire

Sapphire reaches out,
but she knows she cannot intervene.

**"You don't need to earn balance, baby.
You only need to choose it."**

Tyrael

Tyrael cups his hands around his mouth, yelling:

**"Dad—don't fight it!
Just stand!"**

Justice exhales hard—
and stops resisting.

Instead, he plants his feet
and lets the forces hit him fully.

Not fighting.
Not fearing.
Just **standing.**

The chamber reacts instantly:

The pressure equalizes.
The forces stabilize.
The storm stills.

Justice stands perfectly centered—
not through tension,
but through alignment.

Grey nods.

Dr. Grey

**"Exactly.
Balance is not force.
It is permission."**

Justice looks around.

"Permission for what?"

Grey meets his eyes.

"To exist without breaking."

The light softens.
The shadow calms.
The circle stops spinning.

Justice remains standing in the center.

Stable.
Steady.
Balanced.

Sage speaks the final truth of this part.

Sage

**"When the soul learns balance,
it stops needing armor."**

Sapphire places a hand over her heart.
Tyrael grins.
Grey steps back, satisfied.

And Justice—
for the first time in his life—
feels like he is standing exactly where he belongs.

Part II — The Lies That Tilt the Scale

The Chamber of Equilibrium grows quiet—
too quiet.

Light and shadow stand still on either side of Justice,
no longer swirling,
no longer pushing,
no longer testing.

Which means only one thing:

The real test is about to begin.

Balance isn't maintained by strength.
Balance isn't maintained by calm.
Balance isn't maintained by willpower.

Balance is maintained by **truth**—
and dismantled by **lies**.

The chamber knows Justice has stood his ground.
Now it wants to know if he can stand **his truth.**

The floor trembles.
A ring of symbols lights up beneath him.
The air thickens with something familiar:

Avoidance.
Denial.
Self-protection.
Old patterns.

Sage speaks first—because of course he does.

119

Sage

His voice floats like smoke:

**"Balance collapses not because of chaos…
but because of the lies we tell ourselves
to survive it."**

He gestures toward the shadows.

**"Prepare yourself.
The chamber is ready to expose yours."**

Justice's breath tightens.

Dr. Grey

Grey steps to Justice's left—
the side of logic, precision, and accountability.

**"Do not resist the revelations.
Resistance is what distorts the scale."**

Justice nods, jaw clenched.

"I'm ready."

Grey answers evenly:

**"No.
You are willing.
Readiness comes after impact."**

Sapphire winces at the harshness,
but she doesn't argue.
Grey is almost always right when things get surgical.

Sapphire (Cindy)

She moves to Justice's right,
the side of empathy and emotion.

Her voice shakes slightly.

**"My son…
the lies you learned weren't your fault.
They were what you needed to survive
a world that didn't know how to guide you."**

Justice swallows hard.

She continues:

**"But surviving and living
are not the same thing."**

Tyrael

Tyrael walks right up to the center point
and stands almost shoulder-to-shoulder with his father.

**"Dad…
whatever comes out…
it doesn't change how I see you."**

Justice places a hand on his son's shoulder.

"I know."

And that's when the chamber awakens.

The First Lie Emerges: "I'm fine."

The shadow side of the room twists into a shape—
a dark echo of Justice's posture
from a thousand different memories.

Silent.
Stoic.
Numb.
Pretending not to hurt.

Sage identifies it instantly.

**"Ah.
The most common lie spoken by wounded men."**

Grey folds his arms behind his back.

**"This lie destabilizes the scale
more than any single trauma."**

The shadow-figure speaks.
In Justice's voice.

"I'm fine."

Justice flinches.
Sapphire gasps softly.
Tyrael frowns.

Grey cuts in:

"Correct it."

Justice takes a long, steady breath.

**"No…
I wasn't fine."**

Light floods the chamber
as the shadow shrinks,
condensed by truth.

The Second Lie: "It wasn't that bad."

A new shape forms—
this one wounded,
but minimizing its own pain,
like someone apologizing for bleeding.

Sapphire recognizes it.

Her voice cracks.

**"That's the lie children learn
when adults don't see their hurt."**

The shadow whispers:

"It wasn't that bad."

Justice steps toward it.

His voice is low, steady, remorseful:

**"No.
It *was* that bad.
I just didn't know I was allowed to say it."**

A wave of restoring light ripples across the room.

Sage nods approvingly.

The Third Lie: "I don't need help."

This lie emerges tall, rigid, armored—
the version of Justice who survived alone
because he believed he had no choice.

Tyrael steps forward, glaring at it.

**"But you DO need help.
Everybody does.
That lie almost broke you."**

Justice places a hand on Tyrael's back.

"He's right."

Then he faces the armored figure.

**"I needed help.
And I didn't ask.
Because I didn't think I deserved it."**

The armor cracks.
Light pours through.

Grey murmurs:

"Truth restores equilibrium."

**The Final Lie:

"Taking care of everyone else keeps me safe."**

This one hurts the most.

It appears as the version of Justice
who became the emotional protector—
the one who absorbed everyone's chaos,
everyone's grief,
everyone's storms
to keep the peace.

Sapphire sobs softly.

"You learned that from me…"

Justice shakes his head.

**"I learned it from life.
But I carried it too far."**

He steps toward the protector-version of himself.

**"Keeping everyone else balanced
made me disappear."**

He breathes deeply.

**"I don't need to hold the world still
to feel safe."**

The protector-figure dissolves into light
like dust carried by wind.

The Chamber's Verdict

The rotation stops.
The forces calm.
The shadows withdraw.
The light settles.

For the first time,
the scale of the chamber is perfectly still.

Grey steps closer.

Dr. Grey

"Balance is established."

Sage lowers his head.

Sage

"Truth has corrected the tilt."

Sapphire wipes her tears.

Sapphire

**"My son is standing in the middle,
where he always belonged."**

Tyrael hugs Justice's arm tightly.

Tyrael

"We did it."

Justice exhales—
not with relief,
but with alignment.

**"I finally understand it...
Balance isn't a place.
It's a law.
And now...
I'm ready to live by it."**

The chamber glows gold.

Balance is achieved.

Part III — The Center That Moves With You

Balance isn't a destination.
Balance isn't a room.
Balance isn't a silent moment where everything stops hurting.

Real balance is the ability
to **carry truth through motion**
without losing yourself.

The Chamber of Equilibrium knows this.
That's why it never stays still for long.

As soon as Justice breathes into the newfound stillness—
the world shifts.

The floor rotates again.
Not violently this time—
naturally,
like the turning of a planet.

The four around him tighten their circle.

This isn't another confrontation.
This is the application.

The test of movement.
Of life.
Of what happens after the healing.

Justice

He feels the floor moving beneath his feet.

Instead of bracing,
instead of stiffening,

instead of preparing for impact,
he does something new:

He allows it.

**"Life doesn't stop moving.
So balance can't either."**

Grey nods slowly.

Dr. Grey

**"Correct.
Stability is not rigidity.
It is flexibility governed by truth."**

He walks along the moving lines, his steps exact.

**"This chamber is teaching you
how to remain centered
while the world changes around you."**

The rotation speeds up—
not chaotic,
but challenging.

Justice breathes deeper.

Sage

Sage floats above the moving circle,
his form gliding with each rotation,
neither resisting nor controlling.

**"The universe is in constant motion.
Balance is not stillness—
it is your relationship to the changing forces."**

He drifts lower,
speaking directly to Justice.

**"There will always be storms.
There will always be shifts.
There will always be demands."**

His eyes sharpen.

**"Your task is not to eliminate chaos.
Your task is to remain yourself
in the presence of it."**

Sapphire (Cindy)

She steps onto the rotating floor,
her movements graceful, balanced, practiced—
the way a woman learns to adapt through decades of life's
harshness.

She offers her hand.

**"Baby…
balance means you stop reacting to everything
like it's your responsibility."**

Justice takes her hand.

She continues:

**"When the world spins,
you don't spin with it."**

Her voice breaks slightly.

**"I never learned this.
I want you to."**

Tyrael

Tyrael jumps onto the rotating floor like it's a playground ride.

He laughs—not in mockery,
but in joy.

"Dad!
Balance is like… skateboarding.
If you're stiff, you fall.
If you move with it, you stay up."

Justice actually laughs—
a real laugh,
one not weighted by apology.

"You're right."

Tyrael grins proudly.

"See? You're learning."

The Shift in Justice

The chamber rotates faster now,
testing not his wounds,
not his guilt,
not his trauma—
but his **adaptability.**

And for the first time,
Justice stops trying to *win* balance
and starts **moving with it.**

His breathing adjusts.
His stance finds rhythm.

His shoulders loosen.
His mind sharpens.

And something extraordinary happens:

The more the room spins,
the more *still* he feels inside.

The center is no longer beneath his feet.
It's inside his chest.

Grey sees it immediately.

Dr. Grey

**"Excellent.
You have located internal balance."**

Sage bows his head.

Sage

**"The balance that moves with you
cannot be taken from you."**

Sapphire wipes her eyes again.

Sapphire

**"I'm watching you stand in a place
I never could."**

Tyrael bumps Justice's shoulder.

Tyrael

"And you're only getting started."

Justice closes his eyes
and speaks the truth that seals the chamber:

**"Balance isn't something I achieve.
It's something I maintain."**

The rotation slows.
The chamber glows.
The circle aligns.

Justice stands firm—
not because the world stilled for him,
but because **he has learned to stand through motion.**

Grey gives the final verdict.

Dr. Grey

"You are ready for the next law."

Sage smiles knowingly.

Sapphire exhales with pride.

Tyrael beams.

Justice nods.

— CHAPTER 5 —
The Burden of Memory

CHAPTER 5
THE BURDEN OF MEMORY

Part I — The Rooms We Lock Behind Us

Memory is not the past.
Memory is **a room**—
built inside the mind,
furnished by emotion,
and locked when the truth becomes
too heavy to carry in daylight.

Justice steps into the next chamber.

This one is darker.
Not dangerous—
but intimate in the way old wounds are intimate.

The walls are lined with doors.
Hundreds of them.
Some glowing faintly.
Some pulsing with pressure.
Some cracked at the edges.
Some rusted shut.

This is the **Archive of Memory**—
the part of the soul where everything that hurts
gets filed away
until a man is strong enough to face it.

And today, Justice is strong enough.

The five arrive with him—
but more careful now,

134

as if they know these rooms
carry the sharpest truths.

Justice

He runs his fingers along the closest door—
a simple wooden one,
familiar in a way he can't yet place.

"I didn't know I had this many."

Grey answers, stepping beside him.

Dr. Grey

**"Most men underestimate
the weight of unprocessed memory."**

He taps one of the doors lightly.

**"Every moment you survived
but did not understand
becomes a locked room."**

Justice exhales slowly.

"And I avoided opening them."

Grey nods without judgment.

**"Avoidance is a strategy.
But it has an expiration date."**

Sage

Sage glides past the doors,
his hand hovering inches above each one,
listening to memories like they're echoing across time.

**"Some rooms contain truth.
Some contain lies.
Most contain both."**

He pauses at a heavy iron door,
eyes narrowing.

**"And some contain the version of yourself
you feared would destroy you if you remembered him."**

Justice's pulse quickens.

Sapphire (Cindy)

She steps close, placing a gentle hand on Justice's back.

**"Baby…
none of these rooms were created because you were
weak."**

Her voice steadies him.

"They were created because you were *alone*."

Her face softens.

"No child should have to face these rooms by himself."

Justice nods,
a quiet ache rising in his chest.

Tyrael

Tyrael steps ahead,
looking at the doors with youthful curiosity
but also with caution.

"Dad…
it's okay if you don't want to open the worst ones right
away."

Justice smirks faintly.

"You're supposed to be the kid here."

Tyrael shrugs.

"Yeah, but I'm the brave one too."

He points at a door glowing faint blue.

"This one doesn't feel… scary.
Maybe start small."

Justice approaches the blue-glowing door.
It hums with a quiet sadness—
not violence,
not trauma,
just… loneliness.

He rests his hand on the door.

It warms under his touch.

Grey gives instruction.

Dr. Grey

"Remember:
you are not entering to relive the memory.
You are entering to reclaim it."

137

Sage adds:

Sage

**"What you reclaim,
stops owning you."**

Sapphire squeezes his shoulder.

Sapphire

**"Go slow.
Go honest.
Go with us."**

Tyrael gives a small nod.

Tyrael

"I'm right here."

Justice inhales—
deep, steady, grounded.

And opens the door.

Inside the First Room

Light spills into the Archive as the door opens.

The room is small,
softly lit,
and filled with echoes—not of violence,
but of **being alone when he shouldn't have been.**

A younger version of Justice sits on a bed,
knees drawn up,

138

eyes tired in the way only a child's eyes can be when he's pretending not to need comfort.

He's not crying.
He's not frightened.
He's just… waiting.

Waiting for someone to notice.
Waiting for someone to ask.
Waiting for someone to care.

Justice's breath catches.

"I remember this."

Grey steps behind him.

Dr. Grey

**"This was the night you decided
you were safer not needing anyone."**

Sage moves beside the child-version of Justice.

Sage

**"Loneliness is not the absence of people.
It is the absence of being understood."**

Sapphire kneels beside the young boy.

Her voice shakes.

Sapphire

**"Oh God…
I didn't know you felt this way."**

139

Justice places a hand on her shoulder.

**"You were fighting your own battles.
I know that now."**

Tyrael walks to the younger Justice
and sits beside him on the bed.

Tyrael

**"Hey…
you didn't deserve this.
You weren't supposed to feel alone."**

The younger Justice finally looks up—
not at them,
but at *his future self.*

Justice meets his gaze.

This isn't a mirror of pain.
This is a reflection of a boy
who built a life on independence
because he had to.

Justice kneels before his younger self.

Justice

"You're not alone anymore."

The room brightens.

The burden lifts.

The door behind them glows gold.

140

Grey gives the final assessment.

Dr. Grey

"First room reclaimed."

Sage nods.

Sapphire wipes her tears.

Tyrael grips his father's hand.

Justice stands taller.

Because the burden of memory
is lighter
when you don't carry it alone.

Part II — The Rooms That Echo Back

The first room shuts gently behind them—
not sealed,
not erased,
but **integrated**.

And as the door closes,
the entire Archive responds.

Lines of light race across the floor.
Other doors shift,
some pulling inward with pressure,
some trembling with emotion,
some pulsing like hearts
that have been waiting decades to be heard.

Justice stands in the center of the hallway,
and for the first time,
he doesn't feel intimidated.

He feels **ready**.

But readiness does not mean ease.

The Archive begins to rearrange—
doors sliding into new positions,
walls folding like pages of a book,
hallways stretching into the distance.

This chamber responds to truth.
And the truth is:

**The deeper the memory,
the louder it echoes when you finally turn toward it.**

The five gather close.

142

Sage

He is the first to speak,
because he always senses the direction before the others can
see it.

**"The Archive has revealed the next room.
Not the darkest one.
But the truest one."**

Justice inhales sharply.

"Show me."

Sage simply turns—
and a door swings into view.

Not glowing.
Not threatening.

Just *heavy.*

Its wood is dark,
its brass handle worn,
its frame marked by fingerprints—
like a thousand moments leaned against it
but never opened.

Tyrael whispers:

Tyrael

"This one feels… sad."

Not afraid.
Not panicked.

Just sad.

The kind of sadness
you teach yourself to ignore
because it feels too familiar to question.

Sapphire (Cindy)

She steps closer, hand over her chest.

Her voice cracks in a confession she never had the space to
speak in life:

**"That door...
is the loneliness you learned
from watching the adults around you struggle."**

Justice looks at her.

She continues:

**"You weren't neglected.
You were *overexposed*
to the weight of our lives."**

Her eyes soften with truth.

**"You learned to carry us
before you learned to carry yourself."**

Justice's chest tightens.
Not with blame—
with understanding.

Dr. Grey

Grey steps forward,
examining the door like it's a mathematical problem.

**"This room holds
the emotional labor
you performed as a child."**

He speaks calmly, analytically—
but not without empathy.

**"Children are not built
to stabilize the emotions of the adults around them."**

Justice nods.

"But I tried."

Grey meets his eyes.

**"You succeeded.
And that is where the damage formed."**

Sage

Sage floats nearer, fingertips brushing the door.

"This is the room of premature responsibility."

The door hums—
as if agreeing.

The Door Opens

Justice rests his hand on the brass handle.
It's warm—
like the memory has been waiting.

He opens it.

Light spills through cracks in the wood,
but the room inside is dim,
like an overcast day.

In the center,
a younger Justice sits on the floor,
back pressed against a wall,
listening through a closed door
to adults arguing in muffled voices.

He isn't crying.
He isn't frightened.

He just feels responsible.

That is the wound.

He believed the world's storm
was somehow **his to fix**.

Justice steps inside.
The younger version doesn't look up—
he's too focused on the argument behind the door.

Grey speaks quietly.

Dr. Grey

**"This is the moment
you decided to become the peacekeeper."**

Sapphire closes her eyes.

**"You saw pain in others
and believed your job
was to absorb it."**

Sage flips a hand,
and the room becomes clearer—
the ambiance lifting like fog.

Sage

**"Children mistaken for adults
learn to silence their own needs."**

Tyrael steps beside the younger Justice
and sits next to him.

Tyrael

**"You didn't do anything wrong.
You were just little."**

The child version blinks,
finally registering another presence.

Justice approaches him slowly.

He crouches down.

Justice

Soft, steady, gentle.

**"You didn't have to fix anything.
That was never your job."**

The young Justice swallows,
uncertain.

**"But if I don't fix it...
who will?"**

Justice smiles painfully.

**"The adults.
Not you."**

He touches the child's shoulder.

"You were allowed to be a kid."

Grey adds:

Dr. Grey

**"Responsibility without power
is trauma."**

Sapphire kneels, voice trembling.

Sapphire

**"I wish I could go back
and take that weight off your shoulders."**

Sage lifts his hand gently.

Sage

**"Regret does not heal the child.
Recognition does."**

Tyrael wraps an arm around the younger Justice.

Tyrael

"I got you now."

The room brightens.
The walls relax.
The heavy sadness begins to dissolve.

148

Justice takes the younger version's hands in his.

"You don't have to hold the world up anymore."

The boy nods softly.
He stands.

And he steps forward—
into Justice.

Not merging violently,
not fading into light—
but integrating.

A small weight replaced by warmth.

Grey nods in approval.

Dr. Grey

"Second room reclaimed."

Sage smiles.

Sapphire exhales.

Tyrael looks proud.

Justice looks lighter.

But the Archive is not finished.
Three more doors begin to glow.

He looks at the next hallway.

"I'm ready."

And the Archive listens.

Part III — The Room That Was Never Meant to Hold a Child

The Archive rearranges itself
one more time—
slowly, deliberately,
with the gravity of truth that has waited years
for this exact moment.

The doors shudder,
the air thickens,
and a single hallway stretches forward
like a spine of fate.

At the end of it stands *the* door.

Not the most violent.
Not the most dramatic.
Not the most traumatic.

But the **origin**.

The emotional nucleus.
The belief that shaped the blueprint.
The first wound that made all later wounds possible.

This is the room
Justice spent his entire life not opening.

The others feel it instantly.

Justice

He stops breathing for a second,
then forces the air back into his lungs.

"…I know this room."

Grey steps forward, eyes sharp.

Dr. Grey

**"Of course you do.
You built your entire identity around avoiding it."**

Justice doesn't argue.
He can't.

Sage approaches the door like a priest approaching an altar.

Sage

**"This is the memory
that taught you to measure yourself
by the moods of others."**

He places a palm against the wood.
It hums—low, ancient, aching.

**"It is not a monster.
It is a moment."**

Sapphire (Cindy)

She doesn't step forward.

She collapses to her knees—
the truth hitting her like a storm of regret.

**"Please...
please forgive me before you open it."**

Justice rushes to her, lifting her gently.

**"Mom—no.
This isn't about blame."**

151

She shakes her head violently.

"But it *is* about pain you never told me you carried."

Justice cups her face.

**"You were surviving.
I was adapting.
Neither of us knew any better."**

A tear runs down her cheek as she nods.

Tyrael

He moves beside the door,
facing it like a guardian instead of a child.

**"Dad…
I'll go in with you."**

Justice smiles softly.

"I wouldn't go in without you."

The Door Opens

Justice grips the handle.
It vibrates in his hand—
warm and heavy,
as if the memory itself is afraid to be seen.

He opens it.

A quiet room.
A dim hallway.
Not dramatic.
Not cruel.

Just an ordinary moment
that a child wasn't ready to interpret.

A younger Justice—
five, maybe six—
stands in the doorway of a kitchen,
watching a parent (Sapphire) cry at the table.

Exhausted.
Overwhelmed.
Drowning silently.

She doesn't see him.

Not because she doesn't care.
Because she's breaking.

The boy watches her.

Small.
Silent.
Confused.

He takes a single step toward her—
wanting to comfort her,
wanting to fix her,
wanting to understand.

And she—
lost in her own storm—
says without looking up:

"Not now, Justice."

Not sharp.
Not cruel.
Not angry.

Just tired.

But a child doesn't hear "not now."

A child hears:

"Not enough."
"Not wanted."
"Not helpful."
"Not safe to feel."

The belief that shaped his entire life
happened in a single sentence
spoken in exhaustion.

Justice stares at the scene,
breath trembling.

Sapphire covers her mouth, sobbing.

Sapphire

"Oh my God…
I didn't mean—
I never meant—
I was drowning, baby, I was drowning…"

Justice holds her tightly.

"Mom.
It wasn't your fault.
I understand that now."

Sage moves behind the child version,
voice steady.

Sage

**"This was the moment the world taught you
your emotions were burdens."**

He touches the boy gently.

"This is where you learned to silence yourself."

Grey nods, stepping forward.

Dr. Grey

**"And this is the lie
you spent your entire adulthood correcting incorrectly."**

Justice wipes his face.

**"I tried to be everything to everyone…
so no one would ever say 'not now' again."**

Grey replies:

**"Which means this wound
has been dictating your choices for decades."**

Tyrael

Tyrael kneels beside little Justice.

Softly:

**"You thought you had to fix grownup problems…
because you thought not fixing them
meant losing love."**

The child version finally speaks—
his voice tiny, fragile, honest:

"I just didn't want her to hurt."

Justice kneels in front of him,
face softening,
melting.

Justice

**"You were just a little boy.
You weren't supposed to fix anything."**

The child's eyes fill.

"But she was crying."

Justice nods.

**"Yes.
And adults cry.
And it's not your job to heal them."**

He touches the child's cheek.

"It was *never* your job."

The room trembles—
not with fear,
but with release.

Sapphire whispers through tears:

Sapphire

**"I'm so proud of you…
for forgiving me."**

Justice looks at her—
and the forgiveness is already present in his eyes.

156

Integration

The younger Justice stands.
He walks slowly toward his older self.

No fear.
No confusion.
No shame.

He simply says:

"I didn't know I was allowed to be a kid."

Justice answers:

"You are now."

The child steps into him—
becoming warmth, becoming clarity,
becoming **permission.**

The room dissolves.

The hallway brightens.

The Archive opens wider.

And Grey makes the final declaration.

Dr. Grey

**"The core wound has been resolved.
The burden of memory
is no longer directing your identity."**

Sage smiles softly.

Sage

"The boy has come home."

Sapphire rests her head on Justice's shoulder.

Tyrael beams with pride.

Justice breathes—
deep, full, free.

For the first time in his life,
the past stops following him.

Because he has finally
walked back and carried himself out.

– CHAPTER 6 –
Shadows on the Scale

CHAPTER 6
SHADOWS ON THE SCALE

Part I — The Weight That Doesn't Belong to You

Shadows are not evil.
They are **unclaimed truths**.
Pieces of ourselves we pushed aside
because we didn't have the strength,
the language,
or the permission
to carry them.

After the Archive settles,
Justice finds himself standing before the Scale again—
not the cosmic version from the Prologue,
but the **inner scale**,
the one shaped by personal truth,
childhood belief,
and inherited responsibility.

The feather floats on one side.
The other side is empty.

Waiting.

Sage, Grey, Sapphire, and Tyrael form a circle around him.

This chamber is darker.
Not oppressive—
but honest.

The shadows here
are not trying to hide.

160

They are trying to speak.

Justice

He looks at the empty plate.

"I thought I cleared this weight already."

Grey steps forward, calmly correcting him.

Dr. Grey

**"You cleared the memories,
not the shadows they created."**

He gestures at the edges of the room
where faint shapes flicker like half-formed silhouettes.

**"Shadows are the beliefs you adopted
while you were surviving the past."**

Justice nods slowly.

"So these aren't memories."

Grey's voice sharpens.

**"No.
These are conclusions."**

Justice breathes deeper.
He understands instantly:

Pain doesn't disappear
when the memory is resolved.

It echoes
in the beliefs that memory created.

Sage

Sage drifts closer to the shadows,
circling them like a prophet walking through smoke.

**"A man's shadows are not his sins.
They are the truths he learned too soon."**

He touches a dark shape.
It trembles.
Not in malice—
in longing.

**"These are the parts of you
that believed the wrong things
for the right reasons."**

Justice feels something tighten inside him.

Sapphire (Cindy)

She steps beside him, voice thick with emotion.

**"Baby…
these shadows look like guilt."**

Justice nods.

"Yeah."

She continues:

**"Guilt you shouldn't have had to carry.
Guilt that wasn't yours.
Guilt that belonged to the grownups who didn't know
how much you were absorbing."**

Justice closes his eyes.

He knows exactly what room they're entering next.

Tyrael

Tyrael stands beside the feather side of the scale,
kicking lightly at the base.

**"Dad...
shadows aren't monsters."**

Justice looks at him.

Tyrael shrugs.

"They're just things you were scared to say out loud."

Justice exhales.

The first shadow steps forward.

Shadow One: "I caused the pain around me."

It's small—
child-sized—
but heavy.

It looks like a boy
who thought he was the reason
the adults were upset.

Grey identifies it instantly.

Dr. Grey

**"Distorted responsibility.
The belief that you were the cause
of the chaos you witnessed."**

Justice steps forward.

"I wasn't the cause."

Sage confirms.

Sage

**"Correct.
You were the witness."**

Sapphire wipes tears.

Sapphire

"And sometimes the collateral."

Justice reaches out.

The shadow touches his hand—
and collapses into the feathered side of the scale,
losing its weight instantly.

Shadow Two: "I am a burden."

This shadow is larger.
Older.
Sharper.
Built from every moment Justice felt he took too much space,
needed too much,
existed too loudly or too quietly.

Tyrael steps toward this one.

Tyrael

**"Dad.
You weren't a burden."**

164

Justice nods, barely holding his voice together.

**"I know.
But I believed it."**

Grey gestures at the shadow.

Dr. Grey

"Then correct it."

Justice inhales.

**"I am not a burden.
I was a child."**

The shadow flickers—
then melts into light.

**Shadow Three: "If I stop carrying everything, someone
will get hurt."**

This one is the heaviest.

It steps out of the darkness
like a soldier made of fear.

Sapphire's breath catches.

Sapphire

**"That's the protector in you.
The version who kept the peace
because you thought the world would collapse
if you didn't."**

Justice steps toward it.

"I carried too much."

The shadow nods—
as if acknowledging the truth.

Justice continues:

"But it wasn't my responsibility."

Grey stands tall.

Dr. Grey

"Release it."

Justice sets a hand on the shadow's chest
and whispers:

"You don't have to protect me anymore."

The shadow dissolves
like dust in morning light.

The Scale Reacts

The feather glows brighter.

The empty plate lightens.

The room brightens.

Sage speaks softly, reverently.

Sage

**"The shadows have been recognized.
And recognition is liberation."**

Tyrael beams.

166

Tyrael

"One more piece done."

Sapphire wraps an arm around Justice.

Sapphire

"You're lighter, baby."

Grey confirms.

Dr. Grey

**"The scale is nearly balanced.
Shadows no longer distort your truth."**

Justice looks at the scale.
The feather glows softly.
The air is calm.

He is no longer haunted by the shadows.
He's integrated them.

And for the first time,
he feels light enough
to see what comes next.

He steps forward and declares:

"Bring me to Chapter Seven."

And the chamber obeys.

Part II — The Echoes That Refuse to Stay Buried

The chamber darkens—not ominous,
but intentional.
The truth takes dim lighting seriously.

Shadows slide along the floor,
forming shapes that flicker between memory
and belief,
between what happened
and what Justice *thought* happened.

The Scale hums.
The feather glows faintly.
And the second part of this chapter begins.

Justice stands in the circle,
and the shadows around him shift
like old assumptions waking from sleep.

This is the part where the shadows speak back.

The five voices take their places:

- Grey to Justice's left.

- Sapphire to his right.

- Sage drifting above the Scale.

- Tyrael standing near the feather.

- Justice at the center.

The chamber breathes.

And the second wave of shadows emerges.

Shadow Four: "If I show pain, I'll lose love."

This shadow is thin—
almost fragile—
but its presence is suffocating.

It carries a posture Justice knows too well:
straight spine,
tight jaw,
eyes that refuse tears
because tears once made things worse,
not better.

Sapphire's breath catches;
she recognizes it instantly.

Sapphire (Cindy)

Her voice cracks.

**"That's the part of you
that learned love came conditionally.
That you had to be strong
to deserve peace in the room."**

Justice swallows.

"I thought crying would make everyone upset."

The shadow whispers,
in his childhood voice:

"If you cry, they'll leave."

Tyrael steps forward, eyes fierce.

Tyrael

"Dad…
I don't go anywhere when you hurt."

Justice's throat tightens.

Sage speaks next.

Sage

"Vulnerability is not abandonment.
It is invitation."

Grey steps closer.

Dr. Grey

"Correct the shadow, Justice."

Justice touches the shape gently.

"I'm allowed to feel.
And the people who love me will stay."

The shadow dissolves
with a soft hiss
like a truth exhaling.

Shadow Five: "If I'm not perfect, I'm nothing."

This shadow walks forward with rigid posture—
a soldier carved from self-criticism.
It's taller than the others,
heavier,
built from the pressure to be
the strong one,
the provider,

the protector,
the one who never fails.

Sage tilts his head.

Sage

"Perfection is the enemy
of self-acceptance."

Grey adds, clinically:

Dr. Grey

"Perfection is also a trauma response.
A way to control chaos
by becoming impossible to disappoint."

Sapphire steps forward, hands trembling.

Sapphire

"I watched you try so hard
to be more than you needed to be.
And I didn't realize
it was because you felt being yourself
wasn't enough."

Justice steps toward the shadow.

Its voice cracks like breaking glass.

"If I'm flawed,
I'm worthless."

Justice answers quietly.

"Being human isn't a flaw."

The shadow trembles.

**"If I fail…
they'll stop loving me."**

Justice shakes his head.

"Love isn't earned through perfection."

Sage whispers:

Sage

"Set it free."

Justice breathes out:

**"I no longer need to be perfect
to be worthy."**

The shadow shatters.

Shadow Six: "My worth is measured by what I fix."

This one doesn't walk—
it kneels.

Carrying tools made from guilt,
bandages sewn from responsibility,
and eyes heavy with the exhaustion
of trying to repair what was broken
before he ever arrived.

Tyrael frowns.

Tyrael

**"Is that the part of you
that tried to fix everything for everyone?"**

Justice nods.

**"Yeah.
I learned early
that if I didn't fix the room
someone would get hurt."**

Sapphire exhales sharply—
a flash of recognition.

**"That was my weight.
Not yours."**

Grey steps behind the kneeling shadow.

Dr. Grey

**"Responsibility adopted in instability
becomes identity."**

Justice kneels too
so he's eye-level with the shadow.

"You don't have to fix everything."

The shadow shakes its head desperately.

**"If I stop…
everything will fall apart."**

Justice's voice softens.

**"Not anymore.
There are people in my life now
who can carry their own weight."**

Sage raises his hand,
and the shadow loosens its grip
on the imaginary tools.

Justice finishes:

"My worth isn't measured by what I repair."

The shadow dissolves into dust
and the dust turns into light.

The Scale Reacts Again

The feather brightens.
The chamber warms.
The darkness thins.

Grey speaks first.

Dr. Grey

**"Three more distortions removed.
Your inner world recalibrates."**

Sage closes his eyes in calm affirmation.

Sage

"Truth is correcting the imbalance."

Sapphire wipes her eyes.

Sapphire

**"You're letting go
of roles you were never meant to carry."**

Tyrael bumps his father's arm.

Tyrael

**"Dad...
you're getting lighter."**

Justice looks at the Scale.

The feather floats calmly.
The empty plate glows gently.
And Justice whispers:

"I feel it."

Sage answers:

**"Good.
Because the deepest shadow
awaits in Part III."**

Justice nods—steady.

"I'm ready."

The chamber darkens.
Not to threaten—
to reveal.

Part III — The Shadow That Learned to Live Inside You

The chamber goes completely silent.

Not empty.
Not cold.
Not frightening.

Expectant.

This part is not about danger.
It's not about reliving pain.
It's not about confronting something monstrous.

This is the part
where Justice must face
the belief that sat deepest,
quietest,
and longest
in his soul.

The feather glows white.
The empty plate dimly pulses.
The shadows retreat to the edges,
making room for the one shadow
that never truly left him.

It rises from the ground
like darkness gathering itself
into a human shape.

Sage closes his eyes.
Grey stands perfectly still.
Sapphire steps closer but keeps her hands at her sides.
Tyrael grips Justice's arm.

The shadow solidifies.

176

And finally…
it speaks.

Shadow Seven: "I am unworthy of love."

It doesn't shout.
It doesn't accuse.
It doesn't snarl.

It whispers.

A soft, exhausted whisper—
the kind that forms in boys
who learned too early
that being loved came with conditions.

Justice knows this shadow.

He's felt it behind every good moment.
He's heard it in every apology he didn't need to make.
He's carried it in every silence
where he swallowed hurt
just to keep the peace.

This is not the loudest shadow.
This is the oldest.

Justice steps forward.

Justice

His voice is strangely steady.

"You've been here since I was a kid."

The shadow lifts its head,
its face a quiet, wounded version of him—

not broken,
not evil,
just tired.

It answers:

**"I had to be.
Someone had to prepare you."**

Justice's eyes narrow.

"Prepare me for what?"

The shadow gestures vaguely
toward his entire life.

**"For the disappointment.
The loss.
The instability.
The times you were told 'not now.'
The times you felt invisible.
The moments love didn't look like love."**

Its tone cracks.

**"If you didn't expect love,
you couldn't be hurt by losing it."**

Sapphire's breath stops.

Sapphire (Cindy)

She steps forward, voice breaking.

**"Sweetheart...
you learned that because *I* was drowning."**

Justice shakes his head gently.

**"Mom...
this isn't blame."**

He faces the shadow again.

**"You tried to protect me...
but you didn't protect me.
You buried me."**

The shadow flinches.

**"If you believed you deserved love,
you would have been hurt even more."**

Grey steps in.

Dr. Grey

Tone clinical, but compassionate.

**"This belief is the root distortion.
It taught you to accept less than you needed
and give more than you had."**

Sage floats closer, eyes glowing softly.

Sage

**"This shadow was born
not from cruelty
but from misinterpretation."**

He extends a hand toward the darkness.

**"Love withheld out of exhaustion
is not the same as love withheld by choice."**

Justice whispers:

179

"I didn't know that, back then."

Tyrael steps right up beside him.

Tyrael

"Dad...
you're the most loving person I know."

Justice kneels down,
almost collapsing under the weight of that truth.

The shadow trembles.

It wasn't built to withstand love.
Only fear.

The Confrontation

Justice stands slowly.

He moves toward the shadow—
closer than ever before.

"Listen to me."

The shadow stiffens.

"I don't need you anymore."

Its voice breaks:

"Without me...
you'll get hurt."

Justice steps even closer.

**"Without you...
I'll finally be free to be loved."**

The shadow recoils as if struck.

"But... I kept you safe."

Justice's answer is soft.

"You kept me small."

Sapphire sobs behind him.
Tyrael holds her hand.
Sage lowers his head.
Grey stands tall, silently proud.

Justice reaches out—

And touches the shadow's hand.

It shatters into a thousand pieces—
not violently,
but like ashes releasing themselves
after holding on too long.

The chamber brightens.

The feather glows gold.

The empty plate lifts.

The Integration

The pieces swirl around Justice—
not attacking,
not clinging,
but dissolving into light
and sinking into his chest.

181

Not to haunt him.
To restore him.

Grey speaks first:

Dr. Grey

**"Shadow distortion resolved.
Your worth recalibrated."**

Sage smiles faintly.

Sage

**"A soul that believes in its own worth
cannot be controlled by its shadows."**

Sapphire steps forward.

Sapphire

**"My son…
you finally let yourself be loved."**

Tyrael beams.

Tyrael

"You're whole now."

Justice closes his eyes,
one hand over his heart.

**"For the first time…
I believe it."**

The Scale balances.

Perfectly.

Silently.

Beautifully.

And Justice steps off the platform,
ready for Chapter Seven.

CHAPTER 7
Voice of the Feather

CHAPTER 7
THE VOICE OF THE FEATHER

Part I — When Light Begins to Speak

The Scale chamber has changed.

Not darker,
not lighter—
but **clearer**,
as if the air itself has finally decided
to stop lying.

This is the first time Justice sees the feather
not as a symbol,
not as a test,
not as a metaphor—
but as **a presence.**

Floating,
glowing,
alive.

It isn't just measuring him anymore.

It's **speaking.**

Not with words.
With direction.

The feather bobs slightly,
drawing Justice's attention.

Grey, Sage, Sapphire, and Tyrael take their positions—
not as spectators,

185

but as witnesses
to what comes next.

The feather turns on its axis
and releases a soft hum
like the beginning of a sentence.

Justice steps closer.

Justice

**"I've passed the shadows…
so why is the feather calling me now?"**

Grey answers—
precise as always.

Dr. Grey

**"Because shadow work reveals what burdens you.
But the feather reveals what *defines* you."**

Justice frowns.

"Defines me?"

Grey nods.

"Your core truth."

Sage

Sage drifts closer to the feather,
circling it like it's an ancient relic.

**"The feather does not measure guilt or pain.
It measures essence."**

186

He tilts his head.

**"Who you are without survival.
Who you are without fear.
Who you are without the past."**

Justice's breath stills.

Essence.

That is the one thing he has never fully understood.

Sapphire (Cindy)

She steps closer,
her presence softer than the feather's glow.

**"Baby...
the feather speaks for the part of you
that was never damaged."**

Justice turns to her.

"Is there really a part like that?"

Sapphire nods, tears forming.

**"Yes.
Your soul came here whole.
Life just buried it."**

Tyrael

Tyrael moves right under the feather's glow,
face upturned, eyes reflecting white light.

187

"Dad…
the feather isn't showing you what's wrong with you.
It's showing you what's *right* with you."

Justice swallows hard.
He isn't used to that.

The Feather's First Word

A soft breeze stirs around the chamber,
though there is no source.

The feather rises higher.
Then lower.
Then turns toward Justice.

And a sound rings through the space—
not a voice,
not a language,
but a vibration that Justice *recognizes*
deep in his bones.

Sage interprets it.

Sage

"It's asking you to speak truth
not about your wounds—
but about your worth."

Grey folds his hands behind his back.

Dr. Grey

"Shadow work reveals what you are *not*.
The feather reveals what you *are*."

Justice steps fully into the feather's glow.

It brightens.
The chamber quiets.

The world waits for his answer.

Justice

He breathes,
feeling a calm he didn't know he had.

"I am worthy of love."

The feather flashes—
white fire in motion.

Tyrael grins.
Sapphire sobs softly.
Sage nods.
Grey remains still, but approval radiates from him.

Justice continues.

**"I am allowed to exist
without carrying everyone else's weight."**

The feather swirls upward like smoke turned to light.

**"I am allowed to feel.
I am allowed to heal.
I am allowed to grow."**

The feather spins faster,
glowing like a star.

And then—

Justice speaks the truth
he never dared to believe until now.

"I am enough."

The feather explodes into radiance—
a silent burst of white-gold light
that fills the entire chamber
and pushes every last remnant of self-doubt
out of Justice's body.

The chamber shifts.

The feather descends again—
but now it glows differently.

Now it is not measuring him.

It is **reflecting him.**

Sage whispers what the feather cannot say.

Sage

**"The feather weighs the soul
not to find fault—
but to reveal truth."**

Sapphire touches Justice's arm.

Sapphire

"And your truth is light."

Tyrael beams.

Tyrael

"Dad...
you said it.
You finally said it."

Grey closes the moment.

Dr. Grey

"Balance without truth is instability.
Truth without self-worth is collapse.
You now possess both."

Justice stands taller.

For the first time in the book,
his soul feels almost weightless.

This is the Voice of the Feather—
and it has only begun to speak.

Part II — The Name the Soul Remembers Before the Mind Does

When the feather finishes glowing,
the chamber doesn't quiet—
it **deepens**.

The air thickens with meaning.
The light becomes warmer.
The ground hums under Justice's feet
as if the entire soul-world
is preparing to reveal
the one truth he has never been able
to put into words.

The feather rises again—
not as a test
and not as a guide,
but as an **oracle.**

Justice instinctively places his hand over his heart.
Sage drifts closer.
Grey stands ready.
Sapphire moves with reverence.
Tyrael watches with wide, electric eyes.

This is the part where the feather
tells a man who he *is*
beneath everything he survived.

The true name.

Not the name given by family.
Not the name shaped by pain.
Not the name defined by guilt, trauma, or expectation.

**The name his soul carried
before the world added its weight.**

Sage

He speaks first,
because only Sage understands
what this moment truly means.

**"Every soul has three names.

One given by the world.
One shaped by survival.
And one whispered by the soul itself—
the name it remembers
even when you forget."**

The feather tilts toward Sage
as if in agreement.

Dr. Grey

Grey steps forward, precise and analytical.

**"This name is not metaphor.
It is identity distilled.
The feather is calibrating
your essence without distortion."**

He interlaces his fingers behind his back.

**"It will show you the part of yourself
untouched by childhood,
untouched by shadows,
untouched by inherited weight."**

Justice exhales shakily.

"So… the real me."

Grey nods once.

"Yes."

Sapphire (Cindy)

She wipes her eyes.

**"Baby…
whatever name comes…
it's the one you were meant to grow into."**

Justice turns to her.

"Have you ever known it?"

She smiles softly.

**"A mother always knows.
But it isn't my place to speak it."**

Tyrael

Tyrael steps forward, hands behind his back,
standing tall like a young prince in a sacred hall.

"Dad…"

The feather glows brighter.

"…don't be scared of it."

Justice kneels to be eye-level with him.

"Do you know what it is?"

Tyrael shakes his head.

**"No.
But I know you're ready for it."**

Justice stands.

The feather descends
until it floats inches from his chest.

Then it releases a soft tone—
one note
pure as truth.

The world goes still.

And the feather begins to reveal.

The Naming Vision

Light pours outward
from the feather into Justice's chest,
rising through his body
like warmth returning to frozen veins.

The chamber transforms:

- The walls dissolve into horizon.

- The floor becomes a river of light.

- The air becomes weightless and holy.

- The feather becomes a sun.

Justice feels his mind quiet.

His chest opens.

His breath deepens.

He hears nothing with his ears.
He hears everything with his soul.

Sage interprets the glow.

Sage

"The feather is stripping away the names others forced upon you."

Grey finishes the sentence.

Dr. Grey

"So the truth underneath can emerge."

The light sharpens into shape—
three radiant lines that converge into one symbol,
hovering before Justice.

Each line represents:

1. **Who he was forced to be.**

2. **Who he believed himself to be.**

3. **Who he actually is.**

They fuse.

The symbol turns.

The chamber hums.

And then—
the feather speaks
in a single resonant pulse of meaning.

Not English.
Not sound.

Identity.

The word forms in Justice's mind
with a clarity so profound
his knees weaken.

He whispers it aloud:

"Bearer of Balance."

The chamber ignites in white fire.

Sage bows his head.
Sapphire gasps.
Tyrael beams.
Grey's eyes soften—
rare, but unmistakable.

Justice stares at the symbol still hovering before him.

Justice

"...that's my soul-name?"

Sage answers reverently:

Sage

**"Yes.
You were never meant to carry the world...
only to balance it."**

Sapphire steps closer, hand trembling as she touches his arm.

Sapphire

**"You always had a wise soul,
even when you were too young
to understand its purpose."**

Tyrael grins, vibrating with pride.

Tyrael

**"Dad…
your soul is literally a scale."**

Justice laughs through a tight throat.

Grey delivers the final interpretation.

Dr. Grey

**"Bearer of Balance:

A soul whose purpose
is to restore equilibrium
to himself and others—
not through force,
but through truth."**

Justice steps into the symbol.
It dissolves into him.
The feather dims to a calm, warm glow.

He feels steady.
He feels alive.
He feels… aligned.

For the first time,
he knows the name beneath his name.

He whispers:

"I am the Bearer of Balance."

The feather ascends,
finalizing Part II.

Part III — How a Man Wields the Truth of His Own Soul

The chamber doesn't return to normal.

It **evolves.**

The walls extend into infinity.
The floor becomes a bridge of warm light.
The feather hovers above Justice's chest—
not as judge,
not as teacher,
but as **companion.**

When the soul-name settles into him,
the world itself shifts to make space
for who he truly is:

The Bearer of Balance.

This part isn't about discovering identity.
It's about **living it.**

Sage descends first, robes drifting like stardust.

Sage

**"A man who knows his soul-name
must learn to wield it."**

Justice looks up.

"How?"

Sage points to the glowing bridge beneath them.

**"By learning the three laws
that govern your essence."**

200

Grey steps forward—
ready to define each one with precision.

Sapphire wipes her eyes,
bracing for the truth she knows will shape her son forever.

Tyrael stands tall,
proud,
steady,
ready.

The feather brightens.

The lesson begins.

LAW ONE — *Truth Before Reaction*

A new glyph burns into the air—
white, sharp, elegant.

Grey explains:

Dr. Grey

**"As Bearer of Balance,
your soul is crafted to neutralize chaos—
not absorb it."**

Justice frowns.

"So I don't take on people's emotions anymore?"

Grey's tone is firm.

**"Correct.
You respond to truth first—
not their tone,**

**not their pain,
not their projections."**

He steps closer.

**"You remain centered
and let others' storms pass around you
instead of through you."**

Sapphire exhales as if a lifetime of guilt releases from her chest.

Tyrael nods with a smile.

Tyrael

**"Yeah, Dad.
You don't gotta fix everybody anymore."**

The glyph sinks into Justice's chest.

He breathes easier.

LAW TWO — *Presence Over Performance*

A second glyph appears—
fluid, circular, glowing warm gold.

Sage interprets:

Sage

**"Your power is not in what you do.
It is in how you show up."**

Justice tilts his head.

"Explain."

Sage smiles, ancient and kind.

**"Balance is restored
not by effort
but by presence."**

He gestures at Justice's posture,
his breathing,
his grounding.

**"When you are aligned,
others align around you."**

Sapphire steps closer, voice trembling.

Sapphire (Cindy)

**"You've always been that way, baby.
A calm in the storm.
Even when you were hurting."**

Justice looks down, humbled.

Grey clarifies:

Dr. Grey

**"Your existence—
not your performance—
creates balance."**

The glyph melts into him like warmth.

He stands taller.

LAW THREE — *Guidance Without Sacrifice*

The final glyph appears—
the brightest of the three,
shaped like a feather resting on a scale.

Tyrael steps forward first this time.

Tyrael

"I know this one."

Justice smiles.

"Tell me."

Tyrael says it simply,
but the chamber trembles with truth:

**"You can help people
without losing yourself."**

Justice's breath stops.

Sage nods with reverence.

Sage

**"Your gift is guidance—
not martyrdom."**

Grey finishes it:

Dr. Grey

**"You are not meant to carry people.
You are meant to steady them
while they learn to walk."**

Sapphire wipes her tears again.

Sapphire

**"My son…
you don't have to break yourself
to make others whole."**

Justice closes his eyes.

The truth lands.

The feather glows.

The glyph sinks into his chest.

And suddenly—
Justice feels it.

Not a burden.
Not a responsibility.

A **calling.**

A clarity so pure
it nearly knocks him off his feet.

He whispers:

"So this is who I am."

Grey responds:

Dr. Grey

"This is who you have always been."

Sage adds:

Sage

"And who you finally remember."

Sapphire touches his cheek.

Sapphire

"I see it in you."

Tyrael grins wide.

Tyrael

"I'm proud of you, Dad."

Justice opens his eyes.

The feather dims to a steady glow,
settling above him like a crown of light.

He takes a breath—
steady, grounded, whole.

"I'm ready for Chapter Eight."

And the chamber shifts,
opening the path forward.

CHAPTER 8

Trial of the Self

207

CHAPTER 8
TRIAL OF THE SELF

Part I — The Door That Only Opens Inward

The chambers Justice has passed through until now—
the Mirror, the Blueprint, the Archive, the Scale, the Feather—
all opened *for him.*
They responded to wounds,
memories,
shadows,
identity.

But this chamber is different.

This one does not open *for* him.

It opens because of him.

The world shifts.

Light folds inward.
Shadows peel away.
The ground becomes a single polished stone floor,
smooth as glass,
black as a starless night.

A tall doorway stands before him,
shining with a faint outline of gold.

There is no handle.
No hinges.
No mechanism.

It is a door that requires one thing:

208

Self.

The four gather behind him.

Grey stands with analytical silence.
Sage floats with quiet reverence.
Sapphire holds her hands together tightly.
Tyrael stands close enough
that their shoulders almost touch.

Justice steps forward.

Justice

"What is this place?"

Sage answers first.

Sage

"The Gate of Self.
The only door in the soul
that cannot be opened by truth,
memory,
or healing."

Justice frowns.

"Then how does it open?"

Grey steps up beside him.

Dr. Grey

"By acceptance.
Not of the past—
but of who you truly are now."

Justice blinks.

"…now?"

Grey folds his hands behind his back.

"Identity realized must become identity accepted."

Sapphire (Cindy)

She steps in front of him,
eyes teary but steady.

"Baby…
you rebuilt the boy.
You integrated the man.
You uncovered the soul."

She touches the door lightly.

"But you haven't accepted
the responsibility
of being whole."

Justice exhales hard.
His heart tightens.

Acceptance is harder than truth.
Harder than memory.
Harder than healing.

Acceptance requires choice.

Tyrael looks up at him, brave as ever.

Tyrael

"Dad…
this isn't about who you were.
It's about who you are now."

Justice kneels beside him.

"Who am I now?"

Tyrael smiles softly.

"Someone I look up to."

Sage places a hand on Justice's shoulder,
gentle as falling dust.

Sage

"You have reclaimed every broken piece of yourself.
Now you must decide
what to do with the complete version."

Justice turns to the door.

It remains still.
Silent.
Waiting.

The Door Speaks Without Sound

Justice reaches out
and places his hand against the gold outline.

A wave of sensation hits him—
not pain,
not fear,
but pure confrontation.

Every version of himself
that ever existed
stirs beneath his skin:

- The boy who felt inconvenient.

- The teen who hardened too early.

- The young man who carried everyone's weight.

- The father who tried to save a world
  he didn't know how to live in.

- The survivor.

- The fighter.

- The shadow-bearer.

- The man who finally found balance.

They all look at him.

Not accusing him.
Not asking him.

Just waiting for him to claim them.

Grey stands tall.

Dr. Grey

"This door will not open
until you accept every version of yourself
as yours."

Justice's throat tightens.

"All of them?"

Grey nods.

"Especially the ones you tried to leave behind."

Sage floats upward, voice echoing with ancient truth.

Sage

"Self-acceptance is not a feeling.
It is a vow."

Sapphire touches his back.

Sapphire

"You don't have to be perfect to be whole."

Tyrael whispers:

Tyrael

"Just be you.
All of you."

Justice places both hands on the door now.

He whispers:

"I accept myself."

Nothing happens.

He clenches his jaw, breath shaking.

He tries again.

"I accept the boy who was lonely."
"I accept the teen who hid his feelings."
"I accept the man who tried too hard."
"I accept the father who didn't give up."
"I accept the soul that's learning to heal."

The door trembles.

Light seeps through the edges.

Justice inhales deeply.

Then says the truth he has avoided his whole life:

"I accept the man I am becoming."

The door explodes in silent gold light,
folding inward like a sunrise breaking open.

A pathway opens beyond it.

The others shield their eyes.
Justice does not.

He stands tall.

Steady.

Whole.

Sage speaks the closing line.

Sage

"The Trial of Self has begun."

Justice steps through.

Part II — The Man You're Afraid to Become

On the other side of the golden door,
there is no floor at first.
No walls.
No horizon.

Just space.

Not empty—
pure.

Gradually, the world takes shape around Justice:

A circular platform of dark stone.
A sky of shifting light.
No visible source.
No clear direction.

This is not the past.
This is not the underworld of memory.

This is the Court of Becoming.

Here, the question is not:

"Who were you?"

but:

"Who are you on your way to becoming—
if you continue as you are?"

The four appear around him—
not above,
not below—
beside him.

Sage to the front-left.
Grey to the front-right.
Sapphire behind his right shoulder.
Tyrael behind his left.

Justice stands at the center.

And the Trial begins.

Sage

His voice carries like wind across an unseen canyon.

"Every soul stands trial
not before the world—
but before its own potential."

Justice looks around.

"So this isn't judgment?"

Sage shakes his head.

"No.
This is *revelation*."

Dr. Grey

Grey steps forward, eyes sharp, hands folded behind his
back.

"The Trial of Self presents possibilities.
The man you could become
if you act from fear...
and the man you could become
if you act from truth."

He glances at Justice.

"Both will feel familiar.
Only one will be yours."

Justice's jaw clenches.

"What do I have to do?"

Grey answers plainly:

"Witness.
Choose.
Commit."

Sapphire (Cindy)

She steps closer, hand on his upper arm.

"Baby…
this isn't punishment.
It's a chance."

Her eyes carry both pride and worry.

"A chance to stop repeating
what broke you."

Tyrael

Tyrael moves in front of him,
face serious for once—
not scared,
just *aware* of the weight of this moment.

"I'm going to see this too, right?"

Justice hesitates.

"Are you sure you want to?"

Tyrael nods.

"I need to know
who you're going to be…
'cause I'm walking behind you."

Justice exhales.

"…Okay."

He puts a hand on Tyrael's shoulder.

The platform hums.

The air thickens.

And the first image begins to form.

The Shadow Future — The Man of Compromise

A figure steps out of the haze.

At first, he looks like Justice—
same eyes,
same build,
same presence.

But something's off.

His shoulders tilt forward under a weight you can't see.
His jaw is tight with unspoken resentment.
His eyes are tired—
not from age,
but from *constant self-betrayal.*

He is surrounded by people,
but none of them really see him.

218

He gives.
He fixes.
He explains.
He smooths everything over.

Externally, he looks like a responsible man.
Internally, he's collapsing.

Justice

He feels his stomach knot.

"…That's me?"

Grey answers without softening it.

Dr. Grey

"One version.
The path where you continue
to sacrifice yourself
to maintain other people's comfort."

Sage floats nearer to the vision.

Sage

"This is the future you
who never learns to say 'no'
without apology."

Sapphire covers her mouth.

Sapphire

"He looks… empty."

The vision-Justice moves through scenes:

- Saying yes when he wants to say no.

- Carrying guilt for things he didn't do.

- Overworking to prove his worth.

- Staying in rooms that drain him because leaving feels selfish.

- Smiling with dead eyes.

Tyrael's face tightens.

Tyrael

"I don't like him."

Justice flinches.

"He's not a bad man."

Tyrael doesn't back down.

"I didn't say he was bad.
I said he doesn't *know himself.*"

Grey nods slightly.

Dr. Grey

"Correct assessment."

The shadow future-Justice is surrounded by people
who depend on his emotional labor,
but none of them truly support him.

He is needed.
He is used.
But he is never nourished.

Justice whispers:

"What did he believe to end up like that?"

Sage answers.

Sage

"That his purpose was to carry,
not to live."

The vision flickers,
holds,
and then slowly recedes.

The Aligned Future — The Man of the Center

The air changes.

It feels lighter.
Cleaner.
Sharper.

A second version of Justice steps forward.

Same body.
Same life.
Same past.

Different center.

He stands tall—
not rigid,

not aggressive—
just *settled*.

His eyes are clear.
Not because life is easy,
but because he has stopped lying to himself.

He listens when people speak,
but their chaos no longer invades him.
He loves deeply,
without erasing himself.
He sets boundaries
without rage or apology.

He carries weight—
but only what belongs to him.

Sapphire

Her voice comes out in a whisper.

"Oh my God…
that's you when you're free."

Justice watches, eyes burning.

This future-him:

- says "no" without guilt.

- says "yes" with his whole chest.

- walks away from what harms him.

- stays where he is honored.

- looks his son in the eyes with nothing to hide.

Tyrael smiles slowly.

Tyrael

"That's my dad."

Justice swallows hard.

"I want to be him."

Grey speaks before emotion takes over.

Dr. Grey

"Then you must understand
the difference between these two futures."

He gestures—
one hand at the shadow future,
one at the aligned future.

"They are not separate destinies.
They are the result of daily choices
based on what you believe you deserve."

Sage's voice follows.

Sage

"When you act from fear,
you become the first.
When you act from truth,
you become the second."

Justice stares at both of them.

The shadow version looks back with hollow eyes.
The aligned version looks back with calm acceptance.

Neither is magical.
Neither is impossible.

They are simply two different results
of the same life
lived under two different beliefs.

Justice

He speaks slowly.

"So this trial isn't about
whether I'm good or bad."

Grey nods.

"Correct."

"It's about whether I'm honest."

Sage smiles faintly.

Sage

"With yourself,
above all."

Sapphire steps closer, hand over her heart.

Sapphire

"I'll love you no matter which version you become…
but I pray you choose the one
who loves himself."

Tyrael grips Justice's hand tight.

Tyrael

"I want the dad who's here, not just holding everything up."

Justice looks from one vision to the other.

He already knows the answer.

But in this chamber,
answers don't count
until they're spoken.

He straightens.

Face steady.
Eyes clear.

"I choose him."

He nods toward the aligned future.

"I choose the version of me
who doesn't abandon himself."

The aligned version steps forward.
The shadow version dissolves into smoke.

The chamber trembles—
not in threat,
in confirmation.

The aligned future-Justice walks calmly toward him,
stops inches away,
and whispers:

"Then start being me now."

He steps into Justice—
not as a fantasy,

not as a prophecy,
but as a standard.

Light cracks across the platform.

Sage closes his eyes.

Sage

"The verdict is in motion."

Grey nods once.

Dr. Grey

"The Trial continues in Part III."

Sapphire exhales through tears.

Tyrael smiles with fierce pride.

Justice stands taller.

The future is no longer something happening to him.

It is something he's choosing.

Part III — The Oath That Changes Everything

The two futures have merged.

Not into a guarantee,
not into a prophecy,
but into a choice
that Justice has finally made:

He will not abandon himself.

The Court of Becoming hums—
stone beneath his feet glowing faintly,
the sky above shifting like slow light over water.

This last part of the Trial
is not about what he *could* be.

It's about what it will cost
and what it will give
to actually become him.

The aligned future-version of Justice
has dissolved into his chest,
but his presence still lingers—
like a roadmap only he can see.

The feather is not here.
The Scale is not here.
The Mirror, the Archive, the Blueprint—
all gone.

There is only Justice,
his four witnesses,
and the path ahead.

Sage

227

He speaks first, voice carrying like a soft drumbeat.

"Every oath has a price."

Justice nods slowly.

"What's mine?"

Sage spreads his hands.

"To live as the man you chose—
the man of the center—
you must give up
every pattern that contradicts him."

The platform brightens beneath Justice's feet,
as if underlining the words.

Dr. Grey

Grey steps forward,
eyes sharp, tone exact.

"We will be specific."

He never deals in vague.

"The cost of becoming the aligned you is this:"
"You will lose the identities
you built around self-sacrifice."
"You will disappoint the people
who only loved you for your compliance."
"You will walk away from rooms
that once defined you."

Justice swallows.

"That sounds… lonely."

228

Grey doesn't flinch.

"Temporarily."

Sapphire (Cindy)

She steps closer, eyes full, voice warm and trembling.

"You've been loyal to your pain
longer than most people are loyal to their healing."

She touches his arm.

"You will have to break up
with your own suffering."

Justice almost laughs—
because it sounds ridiculous
and absolutely true.

"I've been using pain as proof I'm trying."

Sapphire nods.

"You don't need to suffer
to prove you're serious about becoming better."

Tyrael

Tyrael comes around to stand in front of him,
eyes locked on his.

"Dad…
some people are gonna fall away
when you start loving yourself different."

Justice's chest tightens.

"I know."

Tyrael shrugs, simple and wise.

"Good.
Then there's more room for the ones who stay
because they see the real you."

Justice smiles despite himself.

"How'd you get so smart?"

Tyrael grins.

"Look who I'm learning from."

The Cost, Spoken Plain

The Court responds to honesty.

Symbols begin to rise from the floor—
each one a word,
each word a cost.

They rotate slowly around Justice:

PEOPLE.
PATTERNS.
PLACES.
PERSONAS.

Grey names them.

Dr. Grey

"PEOPLE:
You will release those who only accept you
when you are small."

One symbol fades into his chest.

"PATTERNS:
You will no longer use chaos
as proof you're needed."

Another sinks.

"PLACES:
You will leave environments
that demand your silence."

A third dissolves into light.

"PERSONAS:
You will stop performing strength
and start embodying truth."

The last one melts into him.

Justice breathes—
a slow, deep, *real* breath.

"And what do I gain?"

Sage smiles.

The Reward, Finally Named

Sage

"You gain yourself."

Justice waits.

Sage continues.

"You gain the ability
to walk into any room
and not abandon who you are."

He gestures at the platform.

"You gain peace that is not based on control,
but on acceptance."

Sapphire adds her own answer.

Sapphire (Cindy)

Her voice softens, full of something new:
relief.

"You gain a life
where you are not always on trial."

She smiles sadly.

"Not in your own mind,
not in anyone else's."

Tyrael steps closer, voice firm.

Tyrael

"You gain time, Dad."

Justice looks at him.

"Time?"

Tyrael nods.

"Yeah.
Time you used to spend beating yourself up.
Now you get to use it to live."

Justice's eyes sting.

Grey, for once, lets warmth into his tone.

Dr. Grey

"You gain clarity.
Clarity in your relationships.
Clarity in your decisions.
Clarity in your purpose."

He pauses.

"And you gain the ability
to guide others
without destroying yourself in the process."

Sage's voice takes on that low, prophetic note.

Sage

"As Bearer of Balance,
your presence will become medicine
for those ready to face their own truth."

He leans forward slightly.

"But you must never again
use your own soul
as the sacrifice."

Justice nods slowly.

"No more self-sacrifice as proof of love."

The Court brightens—
as if that one sentence
just rewrote his entire story.

The Oath

A final symbol rises from the floor—
a scale with a feather on one side
and a beating heart on the other.

Justice knows what this is
before anyone explains it.

Sage gestures to it.

Sage

"Speak your oath."

Grey adds, more gently than usual.

Dr. Grey

"Not to us.
To yourself."

Sapphire steps back, giving him space.
Tyrael does too.

Justice stands alone in the center—
not abandoned,
but honored.

He places his hand over his chest,
and speaks slowly,
clearly,
without flinching.

"I will not abandon myself to be loved."
"I will not shrink myself to be accepted."
"I will not carry what is not mine to hold."
"I will live as the Bearer of Balance—
honest, present, and whole."

He takes a deeper breath.

"I will be the man my son can follow
without inheriting my wounds."

The symbol explodes into light
and pours into him.

The Court of Becoming shakes—
not in violence,
but in completion.

Sage closes his eyes.

Sage

"The Trial of Self is concluded."

Grey nods.

Dr. Grey

"Verdict:
You are no longer living under the sentence of your past.
You are living under the oath of your choosing."

Sapphire wipes her face, smiling through tears.

Sapphire

"I finally get to see you as yourself."

235

Tyrael throws his arms around him.

Tyrael

"And I finally get the dad
who knows he deserves to be here."

Justice holds him tight.

For the first time,
the future doesn't feel like a punishment to outrun
or a test to pass.

It feels like something
he is worthy of living.

The Court fades.
The platform dissolves.
The light narrows into a single path ahead.

Justice steps forward.

Balanced.
Awake.
Committed.

CHAPTER 9
The Sacred Middle

237

CHAPTER 9
THE SACRED MIDDLE

Part I — Where Extremes Finally Let Go

The first thing Justice notices
is that there is no chamber.

No walls.
No doors.
No ceiling.
No glowing glyphs,
no heavy symbols,
no cosmic architecture.

Just a horizon.

Soft.
Even.
Endless.

The ground beneath his feet is neither light nor dark—
a muted, warm grey that feels like standing in the pause
between inhale and exhale.

This place is not dramatic.
Not intense.
Not explosive.

It's quiet.

After everything he's passed through—
the Mirror, the Blueprint, the Archive, the Scale, the Feather,
the Trial—
this space feels almost... underwhelming.

But the soul doesn't waste design.

If it's simple,
it's because something important is happening.

The four join him.

Sage appears first, as always in places that feel like
thresholds.
Grey follows, hands clasped.
Sapphire arrives with a softened presence,
no storm behind her eyes—just warmth.
Tyrael steps up beside his father, close, grounded.

Justice turns slowly in a full circle.

"What is this place?"

Sage

His voice is soft,
but it carries easily in the quiet.

"This is the Sacred Middle."

Justice frowns.

"The middle of what?"

Sage smiles just a little.

"Everything."

He lets the word settle.

Dr. Grey

Grey steps to Justice's left,
examining the horizon with analytic eyes.

**"The Sacred Middle is not indecision.
It is not apathy.
It is not 'playing both sides.'"**

He looks directly at Justice.

**"It is the place where you choose to live
outside of extremes."**

Justice tilts his head.

"You mean… not going all-in on suffering or escape?"

Grey nods.

**"Precisely.
The Sacred Middle is where you operate from balance
instead of from panic or numbness."**

Sapphire (Cindy)

She moves to Justice's right,
her hand brushing his arm.

**"Baby…
you've lived most of your life in extremes."**

Her tone isn't accusing—
it's acknowledging.

**"All or nothing.
Give everything or disappear.
Carry it all or collapse."**

She looks at the soft horizon.

240

"This is the place your soul has been trying to lead you to your whole life."

Tyrael

Tyrael squints at the empty expanse.

"So... it's like the middle of the see-saw?"

Justice glances down at him, a half-smile creeping in.

**"Yeah.
The point in the middle where it doesn't slam either side."**

Tyrael nods, satisfied.

"That's where you can actually *stand*."

Sage chuckles under his breath.

"The child is not wrong."

The Middle Is Not "Halfway"

Justice walks a few steps forward.
Nothing changes.
The horizon doesn't move.
The ground doesn't shift.

It feels strangely... stable.

"It doesn't feel like anything," he admits.

Grey answers.

**"That is because you are used to intensity
as proof that something matters."**

241

Justice freezes.

"...Say that again."

Grey obliges.

**"You were taught to confuse emotional extremes
with importance.
If it didn't hurt or overwhelm you,
you didn't think it was real."**

Sage adds:

**"The Sacred Middle will feel flat at first
because it is calm,
not chaotic."**

Sapphire nods, pain flickering in her eyes.

**"We raised you in a storm.
Calm feels suspicious when all you've known is wind."**

Justice looks around again.

The quiet feels less empty now.
More like… rest.

Justice

**"So this isn't the middle between 'good' and 'bad'…
it's the middle between overreacting and shutting down."**

Sage smiles.

"Exactly."

Grey elaborates.

**"The Sacred Middle is not compromise of truth.
It is clarity without panic."**

The Two Roads Justice Used to Live On

Without warning,
two thin lines of light appear in the distance,
stretching out in opposite directions from where he stands.

One road burns bright white—
harsh, sharp, rigid.
The other is deep black—
soft, heavy, consuming.

Justice stares.

"What are those?"

Sage gestures to the white road first.

Sage

**"This is the road of overcompensation—
over-giving,
over-explaining,
over-apologizing,
over-performing."**

Grey continues seamlessly.

Dr. Grey

**"The path where you tried to earn safety
by being flawless,
helpful,
selfless to the point of self-erasure."**

243

Justice watches flashes of his own life play along the white line—
late nights trying to fix everyone else's chaos,
conversations where he swallowed his anger,
moments where he said "it's fine" when it wasn't.

His stomach tightens.

Sage gestures to the black road.

Sage

**"And this is the road of collapse—
shutting down,
numbing out,
disappearing from yourself
because feeling everything became too heavy."**

Sapphire's eyes glisten.

**"The moments where you went quiet.
The ones where you weren't *here* even when you were in the room."**

Justice sees those flashes too—
the nights he checked out,
the days he moved like smoke through his own life.

Tyrael's voice is soft.

Tyrael

"I've seen both."

Justice looks at him, guilt creeping in.

Tyrael shakes his head gently.

244

**"I'm not mad.
I just… don't want you stuck on either road anymore."**

Standing Where Neither Road Owns You

Justice looks down.

The place where he stands—
this soft grey—
is exactly between the two roads,
but not *of* them.

He's not on the white path of overcompensating.
He's not on the black path of disappearing.

He's… here.

Present.
Grounded.
Untied to either extreme.

Grey's tone softens—rare, but real.

Dr. Grey

**"The Sacred Middle is the space
where you can see both roads
without being pulled by either."**

Sage adds:

**"Where emotion is felt
but not obeyed blindly.**

**Where thought is used
but not used to strangle feeling."**

Sapphire smiles sadly.

**"Where you don't have to be the hero
or the ghost."**

Justice closes his eyes for a moment.

"What do I actually *do* here?"

Tyrael answers first, simple and brilliant.

Tyrael

"You *pause.*"

Justice opens his eyes.

"Pause?"

Tyrael nods.

**"Yeah.
Before you go running down either road.
Before you go save everybody or disappear.
You stop here and ask—
'What's true?
What's mine?
What do I really want to do?'"**

Sage grins.

**"Your son has just described
the practice of a regulated soul."**

Grey nods in approval.

**"The pause is the proof
that you are no longer controlled by your old survival
patterns."**

The Sacred Middle as Practice, Not Place

The horizon flickers gently,
as if agreeing.

This isn't a one-time revelation.
It's a **skill.**

Justice looks at the two roads one last time.

He doesn't feel the same pull.

The white road no longer feels like duty.
The black road no longer feels like relief.

Here—
in the middle—
he feels something new:

Choice.

Not frantic.
Not rushed.
Not desperate.

Just… choice.

He speaks it aloud:

**"I don't have to run to either extreme
to prove I care or to escape what I feel."**

The ground glows softly under his feet.

Grey answers:

**"Correct.
You can stay here.
Respond from here.
Live from here."**

Sage finishes the thought.

**"The Sacred Middle is not where you avoid life.
It is where you finally live it."**

Sapphire wipes a tear and smiles.

**"It's where I always wanted you to end up.
Somewhere you can breathe."**

Tyrael bumps his father's hip lightly.

"And it's where I like you best."

Justice laughs—
not forced,
not defensive.

Real.

He takes a deeper breath than the chamber has heard yet.

The Sacred Middle absorbs it easily.

This is where his next decisions will be made.
Not from fear.
Not from old scripts.

From center.

Part II — When Old Triggers Test New Balance

The Sacred Middle doesn't stay abstract for long.

Balance is useless
until it touches **real life**.

The horizon shivers.
The soft grey beneath Justice's feet ripples—
and the space around him begins to **project**.

Not memories.
Not fantasies.

Triggers.

Situations that used to drag him straight
into one extreme or the other.

- Overcompensate.

- Or disappear.

This time,
the Middle is watching.

So are the four.

Grey stands at his left, observant.
Sage floats slightly above and ahead.
Sapphire rests just behind his right shoulder.
Tyrael is at his side, like a small anchor.

The first test arrives.

Trigger One — Disappointment in the Room

249

A scene forms in front of Justice
like a stage being built out of light:

A kitchen.
A phone on the table.
A voice on the other end—
sharp, tired, disappointed.

"You said you'd be there."
"I can't count on you."
"Same old story."

Justice feels it in his chest.
That old reflex.

Fix it. Overpromise.
Take the blame.
Forget your limits.

His weight shifts unconsciously toward the bright "white"
road—
the old path of overcompensating.

Sage sees it immediately.

Sage

"Careful.
You're already leaning."

Justice stops.
Literally—he freezes mid-step.

Justice

"This is where I'd usually say, 'You're right, it's all my
fault. I'll do whatever you need.'"

250

Grey nods.

Dr. Grey

"And abandon your own truth in the process."

Sapphire speaks softly.

Sapphire (Cindy)

**"You're not a bad man
because you can't be everything to everyone."**

Tyrael tugs his sleeve.

Tyrael

**"Ask the questions first, Dad.
Not the apologies."**

Justice breathes.

The Sacred Middle hums under his feet
as he imagines how he will respond.

He speaks into the scene—
not to win,
not to appease,
but from center.

**"You're allowed to be disappointed.
But it isn't true that I'm 'never there.'
I'm doing my best within what I can really give."**

The phone-voice tightens, then quiets.
The scene wavers.

Justice adds:

"I won't agree to things I can't actually do just to make you feel better in this moment. That's not fair to either of us."

The old urge to fix everything
tugs at him once—
then fades.

The scene dissolves.

The white road dims slightly,
as if losing some of its pull.

Dr. Grey

"You stayed in the Middle. You told the truth instead of buying guilt."

Sage nods.

Sage

"The Sacred Middle survived contact."

Tyrael grins.

Tyrael

"One for one."

Trigger Two — The Urge to Disappear

The horizon shifts again.

New scene.

A crowded day.
Too many demands.
A dozen emotional weights at once:

- Someone needs money.

- Someone needs advice.

- Someone wants his time *now*.

- His own body is tired.

- His mind is loud.

In the past, this was the point
where his system would overload and flip
into **shutdown**.

Scroll.
Numb.
Vanish.

The dark road—the old collapse path—
glows invitingly at the edge of his awareness.

Just disappear,
it whispers.
They'll figure it out. You don't matter anyway.

Justice feels the pull.

His shoulders want to sag.
His chest wants to cave in.
His energy wants to drop straight through the floor.

He almost steps toward the black road.

Tyrael's small hand grabs his.

Tyrael

**"Hey.
Don't leave."**

Two words.
They hit harder than any lecture.

Sapphire steps closer.

Sapphire

**"You used to disappear like that as a boy.
You thought it protected you."**

Grey's voice is low, precise.

Dr. Grey

**"Withdrawal is a form of self-defense.
But taken too far, it becomes self-erasure."**

Justice closes his eyes.

He breathes.
Once.
Twice.

He chooses the Middle.

"I'm overwhelmed."

Just saying it
shifts the entire scene.

He continues:

**"I can't handle all of this at once.
I need to step back,
not vanish—
and come back with intention."**

In the projected scene,
some people understand.
Some don't.
Some push.
Some back off.

But the important thing is this:

Justice doesn't disappear from **himself.**

He stays.

On the grey ground.
In his own body.
With his own truth.

The dark road dulls.

Sage

**"Good.
You didn't abandon your post
inside your own life."**

Grey adds:

Dr. Grey

**"The Sacred Middle is not neutral.
It is an active stance."**

Tyrael squeezes his hand.

Tyrael

"That's two."

Justice exhales, a little steadier now.

Trigger Three — Internal Shame, No Audience Needed

The third test doesn't appear as a scene.

There is no room.
No other person.
No phone.

Just… a voice.

His.

It rises uninvited from the old wiring:

"You should be further by now."
"You've wasted too much time."
"Any other man would have done more with this life."

There are no external triggers.
This is just the echo
of every old standard
he used to beat himself with.

No white road appears,
no black.

Because shame doesn't need a road.

It lives in the **head**.

Justice's jaw clenches.

"Yeah. There it is."

Grey's eyes narrow slightly.

Dr. Grey

**"This is the hardest test.
The world isn't accusing you.
Your own narrative is."**

Sage floats lower.

Sage

**"Remember:
not every thought that sounds like you
belongs to you."**

Sapphire steps in front of him,
eyes fierce through the softness.

Sapphire

**"You were always too hard on yourself.
Harder than any of us were.
Harder than the world was."**

Tyrael steps directly into his line of sight.

Tyrael

**"Would you let somebody talk to me
the way you talk to you?"**

Justice stops cold.

He answers without thinking:

"Never."

Tyrael doesn't blink.

"Then why do you let you?"

Silence.

The Sacred Middle feels heavier now—
not with burden,
with **honesty.**

Justice straightens.

He doesn't fight the shame.
He doesn't obey it either.

He **talks back.**

Justice

**"I haven't wasted my life.
I've survived it."
"I'm not behind.
I'm arriving."
"Any other man would have broken
under some of the things I carried."**

He takes a deeper breath.

**"I am not in competition with who I 'should' be.
I'm committed to who I'm becoming."**

The accusations weaken.
They don't vanish forever—
but they lose their authority.

Sage smiles.

Sage

**"You just moved the courtroom
out of your head
and back into your soul."**

Grey nods once, satisfied.

Dr. Grey

**"You responded from the Middle—
not from shame,
not from ego."**

Sapphire's shoulders drop in relief.

Tyrael grins.

Tyrael

"Three for three."

Justice looks around.

The horizon is calm.
No roads burning,
no shadows reaching for him.

Just space.

Space where he can choose.

He realizes something quietly:

"This... is sustainable."

Not dramatic.
Not addictive.

Sustainable.

The Sacred Middle hums under his feet,
as if agreeing.

Part III — Turning a Place Into a Way of Living

The tests fade.
The projections dissolve.
The roads dim.

What's left is simple:

Justice.
The horizon.
The soft grey ground beneath his feet.

And a feeling he's never really had before:

This is somewhere I can stay.

Not as a perfect man.
Not as a finished story.
But as someone who finally knows
how not to abandon himself.

The Sacred Middle hums quietly—
not like a machine,
but like a heartbeat.

The four move closer.

This isn't a trial now.

This is a briefing.

A way of life.

Justice

He looks around at the calm horizon.

"So this isn't just a chamber I visit.
This is how I'm supposed to *live*."

Grey nods once.

Dr. Grey

"Correct.
The Sacred Middle is not a location.
It is a posture."

He gestures at Justice's stance.

"This is your new default.
You return here before you respond.
Before you react.
Before you decide."

Sage smiles faintly.

Sage

"The Middle is your home base.
You may visit extremes,
but you do not *live* there anymore."

Sapphire (Cindy)

She exhales, a long, tired breath
that sounds like she's been waiting his whole life
for this exact moment.

"Baby…
for years you thought being calm meant you didn't care
enough."

She shakes her head.

**"You care deeply.
You just don't have to destroy yourself to prove it."**

Her eyes soften.

"This is where you can care and stay whole at the same time."

Tyrael

Tyrael rocks on his heels.

**"So, like…
if life's a game,
this is your spawn point."**

Justice laughs.

**"Yeah.
Every time the world knocks me around,
I respawn here."**

Tyrael grins.

"Exactly."

How the Middle Works in Real Life

The horizon flickers again,
but this time it doesn't show full scenes—
just flashes.

Everyday moments.

The kind that used to slip by unnoticed
while old patterns ran the show.

Now the Middle is watching.

Flash One — The Message

A text buzzes in front of him:

"Hey, can you talk? I really need you. It's important."

Old reflex:
Drop everything.
Forget his own exhaustion.
Overgive.

New Middle-rule:

Justice breathes.
Checks in with himself first.

"Can I really hold space right now?"

In the Sacred Middle,
he hears his own answer clearly:

I'm tired. I can talk, but not for an hour. I have limits tonight.

He responds from there:

**"I've got some energy, but not a lot.
I can give you 15–20 minutes right now,
or a deeper talk tomorrow.
Which do you prefer?"**

He stays present.
He stays honest.
He stays **whole.**

The Middle hums.

Flash Two — The Temptation to Spiral

An image of himself passes—
late at night,
laying in bed,
mind wanting to wander into:

"You failed.
You're behind.
You should be more by now."

Old reflex:
Let the spiral run the show.
Believe every thought that hurts.

New Middle-rule:

Pause.
Return.

From center, he says to himself:

"These thoughts feel familiar,
but they aren't the whole truth."

"I'm moving.
I'm growing.
I've survived a lot."

He doesn't argue with every lie.
He just doesn't surrender to them.

The spiral weakens.

The Middle holds.

Flash Three — The Moment With His Son

A final flash:
Justice with Tyrael in the real world—
not in a chamber,
not in soul-space.

Just a regular day.

Tyrael asks a question
at a bad time:

"Dad, can we talk about something?"

Old reflex options:

- Overcompensate: force himself to talk,
  even if his brain is fried.

- Disappear: say "later"
  and never come back.

New Middle-rule:

He checks in with himself first.
Checks his energy.
Checks his honesty.

Then:

**"Yeah. I want to.
But if we do it right now,
I won't be fully present.
Give me 20 minutes to finish this,
and then I'm all yours.
And if I forget—
remind me. I *want* that talk."**

Tyrael in the vision smiles—
not because his dad is perfect,
but because his dad is **real.**

The flash fades.

The horizon returns.

Each Voice's Role in the Middle

The Sacred Middle stabilizes beneath him
as the four step closer for something like a vow—not formal,
just *true*.

Dr. Grey

"I'll guard your clarity."

**"When fear tries to impersonate logic,
I'll help you separate them."**

**"When you're tempted to over-explain,
I'll remind you:
truth doesn't need a sales pitch."**

Sage

"I'll guard your perspective."

**"When you forget how far you've come,
I'll show you the map."**

**"When you think a moment is everything,
I'll remind you it's only a chapter."**

Sapphire (Cindy)

"I'll guard your heart."

**"When you start talking to yourself
the way the world talked to you when it was tired,
I'll remind you:
you deserve gentleness too."**

**"When you feel like a burden,
I'll remind you that your existence
has always been a blessing."**

Tyrael

He grins, then speaks with unexpected weight.

"I'll guard your legacy."

**"When you want to go back to being small,
I'll remind you that I'm watching
how you treat yourself."**

**"When you're tired of trying,
I'll remind you why you started."**

Justice looks at all of them.

Then looks at where he's standing.

Justice

**"So this is it.
This is my new normal."**

Sage nods.

Sage

**"The Sacred Middle is not glamorous.
It will not always feel exciting.
It will often feel simple,**

**ordinary,
quiet."**

He smiles.

"That's how you know it's real."

Grey adds:

Dr. Grey

**"Your work now is practice.
Repetition.
Returning here a thousand times
until it becomes effortless."**

Sapphire squeezes his arm.

Sapphire

**"And every time you forget,
you can come back without shame."**

Tyrael bumps him lightly.

Tyrael

**"Middle's always here, Dad.
Just like us."**

Justice smiles.

Not forced.
Not performative.

Just… present.

He looks at the horizon one more time
and understands:

He doesn't have to chase balance anymore.

He *is* balance,
learning how to live as himself.

He takes a breath that belongs to **now**
—not the past,
not the future.

"I'm ready to keep going."

The Sacred Middle glows beneath him,
then gently releases him forward.

CHAPTER 10

Forgiveness as Force

271

CHAPTER 10
FORGIVENESS AS FORCE

Part I — What Forgiveness Is *Not*

Forgiveness is one of the most abused words in the human language.

People talk about it like:

- a moral trophy,

- a religious checkbox,

- a polite way to erase history,

- a demand placed on the wounded
  so everyone else can stay comfortable.

Justice was raised inside that confusion.

He heard *"forgive and forget"*
when what they really meant was:
"Pretend it didn't happen so we don't have to change."

He heard *"let it go"*
when what they really meant was:
"Stop making us feel guilty."

He learned to "forgive"
by burying things.

Not healing them.
Just hiding them.

It never worked.

272

The soul does not honor lies,
even when you wrap them in holy language.

So when this chapter begins,
Justice is not in a courtroom,
or a chamber,
or on a scale.

He stands in a vast plain
filled with **threads**.

Black, grey, gold, red—
stretched out across the ground,
running from his chest to distant points in space
he cannot fully see.

Each thread hums with connection.

Some are still.
Some are snarled.
Some are burning slowly.

This is not the past.

This is **every unresolved bond**
between him and the people, systems, and stories
that hurt him
or that he hurt.

The place is quiet.

The weight is not.

Sage, Grey, Sapphire, and Tyrael appear beside him.

Justice

He stares at the threads, uneasy.

"What is this?"

Grey steps forward, eyes cataloguing the lines.

Dr. Grey

"These are your ties."

**"Every time you were wronged
and swallowed it instead of facing it—
a thread."**

**"Every time you hurt someone
and never owned it—
a thread."**

**"Every time you said 'it's okay'
when it wasn't—
a thread."**

Justice's chest tightens.

"So this isn't just about what people did to me."

Grey shakes his head.

**"No.
Forgiveness is never one-directional.
It is the rebalancing of all accounts."**

Sage

Sage glides over the field of threads,
robe brushing lightly against them.

274

Some vibrate.
Some flinch.
None break.

**"These are not memories.
They are *contracts*."**

He lifts a black thread.

**"This one says:
'I will carry the anger
for what you did
for the rest of my life.'"**

He lifts a red one.

**"This one says:
'I will keep punishing myself
for the hurt I caused
even after I've changed.'"**

He lifts a frayed grey thread.

**"And this one says:
'I will pretend it didn't matter
while it eats at me forever.'"**

Justice looks down at his chest.

All of them lead back to him.

Sapphire (Cindy)

She comes closer, hand over her heart.

**"Baby…
this is what happens**

275

**when you confuse forgiveness
with pretending you're not hurt."**

Her voice is gentle,
but it hits like truth always does.

**"You forgave people too quickly in words
because you were scared
they'd leave if you admitted the damage."**

Justice's throat tightens.

"Yeah."

Sage nods slowly.

**"Verbal forgiveness
without emotional honesty
creates threads
instead of healing."**

Tyrael

Tyrael crouches down,
poking one of the threads curiously.

**"So...
these are like...
emotional IOUs?"**

Justice manages a small smile.

**"Yeah.
Promises you never said out loud
but still kept living by."**

Tyrael scrunches his face.

"They look heavy."

Grey answers.

Dr. Grey

**"They are.
You've been dragging them
through every room of your life."**

Justice looks across the field
and realizes
how tired his soul really is.

Not just from what happened to him—
but from never cutting what kept him tied to it.

What Forgiveness is *Not*

The threads hum louder
as if listening for what comes next.

Sage turns to Justice, eyes bright.

**"Before we show you what forgiveness is…
we must strip away what it is *not*."**

Four statements appear in the air,
written in light:

1. **Forgiveness is not forgetting.**

2. **Forgiveness is not reconciliation.**

3. **Forgiveness is not saying "it was okay."**

4. **Forgiveness is not self-erasure.**

277

Grey reads each one out,
voice steady.

Dr. Grey

"Forgiveness is not forgetting."

**"The soul does not heal
by pretending it never bled.
You are allowed to remember
and still release the hold it has on you."**

One of the threads loosens.

"Forgiveness is not reconciliation."

**"You can forgive someone
without ever letting them near you again.
Health does not require repeated harm."**

Another thread relaxes its pull.

"Forgiveness is not saying 'it was okay.'"

**"If it was okay,
forgiveness wouldn't be necessary."**

Justice flinches.

He's said *"it's okay"*
more times than he can count.

"Forgiveness is not self-erasure."

**"If forgiving someone
requires you to disappear,
you are not forgiving—
you are sacrificing."**

The words settle like stones
in the deepest part of him.

Sapphire (Cindy)

She squeezes his arm.

**"You were taught that being a 'good' person
meant making yourself smaller
so others didn't have to face what they'd done."**

Her eyes glisten.

**"That isn't goodness, baby.
That's fear in a costume."**

Justice looks down.

He can see now
how many times he made himself
the apology
for someone else's behavior.

Justice

"So what is forgiveness then?"

Sage smiles—
not softly this time,
but with a kind of fierce brightness.

Sage

"Forgiveness is force."

The threads tremble.

**"It is the decision
to end the contract
that keeps you emotionally owned
by what happened."**

He gestures to the field.

**"It does not excuse.
It does not erase.
It breaks."**

Grey nods.

Dr. Grey

**"To forgive is to cut a thread—
not to pretend it isn't strangling you."**

Tyrael

He looks up at Justice.

"So you're not doing them a favor?"

Sage shakes his head.

**"No.
You're doing your soul a favor."**

Sapphire adds:

**"You're taking your power back
from the moments that took it."**

Justice looks over the field again.

It still stretches far.

It's still overwhelming.

But now,
it doesn't feel like punishment.

It feels like **work**.

Real work.
Necessary work.

Justice

"So this chapter isn't about me being 'nice'."

Grey almost smiles.

**"No.
This chapter is about you becoming free."**

Sage lifts one finger.

**"And we will start
not with the biggest betrayals—"**

He points at a single, thin thread near Justice's foot.

**"—but with the smallest knots
you've left in your own heart."**

Sapphire nods.

**"We start where you *can* move…
and build toward what you never thought you could."**

Tyrael cracks his knuckles, grinning.

**"Okay then.
Let's cut some threads."**

Justice inhales.

For the first time in his life,
forgiveness does not feel like something
being *asked* of him.

It feels like something
he is about to **wield.**

The field of threads hums, waiting.

Part II — Cutting the First Threads

The field of threads hums.

Now that Justice knows what they are,
he can feel them differently:

Not just as **weight**,
but as **agreements**
he never meant to sign.

Some buzz with old anger.
Some with quiet shame.
Some with that numb, familiar ache
he learned to call "it is what it is."

Sage floats above the closest cluster,
eyes half closed, listening.

Grey watches with his hands behind his back,
already building the method.
Sapphire stands close enough to touch him,
but doesn't—she lets him have his space.
Tyrael crouches by a few of the nearest threads,
poking at them like wires waiting to be unplugged.

This is not symbolic anymore.

This is **surgery.**

Sage

He speaks first, voice calm but charged.

**"We begin with the threads
that look light but pull you every day."**

He gestures to a few thin lines
near Justice's feet—
almost invisible,
but buzzing with a low static.

**"Resentments you told yourself were 'no big deal.'
Self-blame you called 'being realistic.'
Moments you laughed off
that still sting under the skin."**

Justice nods slowly.

"How do I cut them?"

Grey steps into place.

Dr. Grey

**"We will use a simple sequence.
Four steps."**

Symbols appear in the air as he names them:

1. **Name the wound honestly.**

2. **Name what it cost you.**

3. **Revoke the contract.**

4. **Release the other person *and* yourself from the role.**

**"No pretending.
No minimizing.
No spiritual bypass."**

Tyrael lifts his head.

284

Tyrael

"So… like uninstalling an app?"

Grey pauses, then inclines his head.

**"An inelegant metaphor.
But sufficiently accurate."**

Sage smirks.

Sapphire almost laughs through her tension.

Justice exhales.

"Alright. Let's uninstall something."

Thread One — The Quiet Resentment

Sage lowers himself beside a thin, grey thread
running from Justice's chest
to a faded figure in the distance—
someone from his past,
more acquaintance than enemy.

"This one," Sage says softly,
**"is the person you always came through for
who never really showed up for you."**

Justice feels it immediately.

The times he answered late-night calls,
helped with crises,
showed up to support—
and when he needed help?

285

Silence.
Excuses.
Last-minute bail.

He'd told himself it didn't matter.

"That's just how people are."
"I shouldn't need anything anyway."

But the thread hums with the friction of the lie.

Step 1 — Name the wound honestly.

Justice kneels and grips the thread.

**"You made me feel like I was only valuable
when I was useful to you."**

**"I pretended I didn't care
that you weren't there for me."**

"But I did."

The thread vibrates harder—
not in anger,
in recognition.

Step 2 — Name what it cost you.

Justice breathes deeper.

**"It cost me trust.
It taught me to expect less
than what I give."**

**"It taught me to stay in one-sided loyalty
because I didn't want to be alone."**

286

Sapphire wipes at her eyes quietly.

Tyrael listens, still.

Step 3 — Revoke the contract.

The words come slower,
but they come.

**"I revoke the contract
that says I have to keep showing up for you
the way you never showed up for me."**

**"I release myself
from the rule that I must accept crumbs."**

The grey thread frays.

Step 4 — Release the roles.

Justice finishes:

**"I forgive you
for not being the friend I needed."**

**"I forgive myself
for staying in a role that starved me."**

He's not pretending it didn't happen.
He's not saying it was okay.

He's cutting the tie.

The thread snaps.
It dissolves into dust,
then into light,
then into nothing.

287

The faded figure in the distance
grows even more distant—
not erased from history,
just no longer plugged into his **now**.

Grey nods.

Dr. Grey

"First thread severed."

Sage smiles.

Sage

"Not bad for a first cut."

Tyrael looks impressed.

Tyrael

"You didn't even flinch."

Justice exhales.

"…I feel lighter."

Sapphire touches his shoulder gently.

**"That's one less weight
you have to drag into every new friendship."**

Thread Two — The Self-Blame Loop

A red thread catches Grey's eye.

Thicker.
Closer.

288

It runs from Justice's chest
straight back **into himself**,
circling like a loop around his ribs,
tight, constricting.

Sage's voice lowers.

"This one is not about someone else."

Grey nods.

**"This is the mistake
you never forgave yourself for."**

Justice already knows which one it is.

Not the single worst thing he's ever done—
but the one that **symbolized** something for him.

A choice.
A failure.
A moment where he didn't live up to his own standard.

He swallows.

Step 1 — Name the wound honestly.

He grips the red thread.

"I hurt someone I cared about."

**"I wasn't as present, honest, or stable
as I should have been."**

**"I disappointed them…
and myself."**

The thread burns under his hand.

289

Step 2 — Name what it cost you.

He doesn't look away.

**"It cost me trust in myself.
It made me doubt my own goodness."**

**"It made me feel like no matter what I do,
I'll always be the guy who messes it up."**

Sapphire's face twists with empathy.

Sapphire (Cindy)

**"You punished yourself longer
than anyone else ever did."**

Justice nods, jaw tight.

Step 3 — Revoke the contract.

His voice shakes,
but it doesn't break.

**"I revoke the contract
that says one version of me from my past
gets to define every version of me after."**

**"I revoke the agreement
that says I must carry this guilt forever
to prove I'm sorry."**

The thread loosens.
Heat fades.

Step 4 — Release the roles.

This is the hardest part.

**"I forgive myself
for who I was back then."**

He pauses, then adds:

"I am not that man anymore."

The loop around his ribs uncoils.

The red thread snaps—
not violently,
but cleanly.

It pulls out of his chest,
leaving a burn that cools into something else:

Space.

Grey nods, more warmly this time.

Dr. Grey

**"Correction:
You are the man who learned from it."**

Sage speaks quietly.

Sage

**"Guilt kept you from becoming him sooner.
Forgiveness makes room."**

Tyrael steps closer.

Tyrael

**"I don't need you perfect.
I just need you *here*."**

Justice lets out a breath
he's been holding for years.

Sapphire smiles through her tears.

**"You were always harder on yourself
than anyone else ever could be."**

He doesn't argue.

Because she's right.

Thread Three — The "It Didn't Matter" Lie

One more.

A thin, frayed thread,
almost completely transparent,
running to a blurry figure in the distance.

Sage touches it.

"This," he says,
**"is something you told yourself didn't matter
because 'other people had it worse.'"**

Justice feels it—
the familiar minimization.

The time someone belittled him.
Dismissed his feelings.
Talked to him like he was less.

He'd laughed it off.

"Whatever. I'm used to it."

But the thread stayed.

292

Step 1 — Name the wound honestly.

Justice grips it.

**"You made me feel small
for having needs."**

**"I told myself it was nothing.
But it chipped at me."**

The thread tightens,
then trembles.

Step 2 — Name what it cost you.

**"It cost me the belief
that my feelings deserve space."**

**"It taught me
to compare my pain
instead of honor it."**

Sage nods approvingly.

Step 3 — Revoke the contract.

**"I revoke the contract
that says I must swallow hurt
because 'other people had it worse.'"**

**"Pain doesn't need to be the biggest
to be real."**

The thread starts to fade.

Step 4 — Release the roles.

**"I forgive you
for not knowing how to talk to me with respect."**

**"I forgive myself
for pretending it didn't matter
when it did."**

The thread dissolves
like mist in sunlight.

A small weight inside his chest
goes with it.

The Field Responds

The ground vibrates softly.

Some of the farther threads
shift on their own,
loosening under the influence
of the first cuts.

Justice looks out over the field.

It's still huge.
There is still so much work.

But something has changed.

It's no longer endless **debt**.

It's a **list**.

A process.
A path.

He isn't drowning in it.

He's moving through it.

Dr. Grey

"You see now.
Forgiveness is action.
Not pressure."

Sage

"We started with the subtle.
Next comes the heavier lines—
the ones tied to family,
betrayal,
abandonment,
injustice."

Sapphire (Cindy)

She takes his hand.

"And I'll be here
when it hurts to remember."

Tyrael

He grips Justice's other hand.

"And I'll be here
to remind you why it's worth it."

Justice looks at the remaining threads.

He doesn't rush.
He doesn't collapse.

He just nods.

"Okay.
Let's go to the deep ones."

The field hums,
preparing for what comes next.

Part III — The Cords That Change the Story

The easy threads are gone.

The field is quieter now—
less static,
less tangled.

But as the surface clutter clears,
the **real weight** reveals itself.

Not threads.

Cords.

Thick.
Dark.
Anchored deep in his chest
and stretching far into the distance—
to family,
to absence,
to the parts of life that were never fair.

The air cools.

The ground hums.

This is the layer of forgiveness
that doesn't feel polite
or pretty
or inspirational.

This is the layer that hurts.

Sage lowers himself closer to the ground.
Grey's posture straightens.

Sapphire takes a slow breath and stands her ground.
Tyrael's face grows serious, but he doesn't move away.

Justice stares at the thickest cord first.

He already knows who it belongs to.

Sage

His voice is softer now,
but heavier.

**"These are not incidents.
They are stories."**

He gestures at the cords.

**"Stories you built your identity around.
Stories that told you who you were allowed to be…
and who you would never escape becoming."**

Grey adds:

Dr. Grey

**"Cutting these cords
does not erase the story.
It changes your role in it."**

Justice nods slowly, throat tight.

**"Okay.
Let's go."**

Cord One — The Father Wound

The first cord is wrapped thick around his chest,
like someone tied a belt around his heart
a long time ago.

It runs outward into the distance—
toward the outline of a man:

Not a monster.
Not a stranger.

His father.

Not as a villain,
but as the man who didn't know
how to show up the way a boy needed.

Justice steps closer to the cord.
It tugs back.

Sapphire inhales sharply.

Sapphire (Cindy)

"This one's been there since you were little."

Her voice trembles.

**"You were always looking for him,
even when you pretended you weren't."**

Tyrael looks up at his dad,
eyes heavier than his age.

Tyrael

**"I've seen that look in you.
Like you're trying to be a dad
without ever having one to copy."**

Justice swallows hard.

He grips the cord.

Step 1 — Name the wound honestly.

His voice is low, but clear.

**"You weren't there the way I needed."
"Sometimes you were absent.
Sometimes you were distant,
or wrapped in your own storms."
"I learned how to be a man
by guessing."**

The cord vibrates—
recognizing itself.

Step 2 — Name what it cost you.

Justice doesn't look away.

**"It cost me trust.
It cost me a blueprint.
It made me feel like I wasn't worth staying for."**

He exhales.

**"It made me terrified
that I'd become you in all the ways that hurt."**

Sage nods slowly.

Sage

"Children who grow up in the absence of a father often raise themselves in the shadow of a ghost."

Grey's tone is clean.

Dr. Grey

**"You built your masculinity
on avoiding his mistakes
instead of knowing your own design."**

Step 3 — Revoke the contract.

Justice closes his eyes.

His grip tightens on the cord.

**"I revoke the contract
that says my worth as a man
is measured by your ability to love me."**

**"I revoke the belief
that I am doomed to repeat your patterns."**

The cord shudders—
some of the pressure around his chest loosens.

Step 4 — Release the roles.

His voice breaks,
but it doesn't stop.

**"I forgive you
for the father you were not able to be."**

**"I release you
from being the standard I judge my manhood by."**

**"I forgive myself
for carrying your failures
as if they were my destiny."**

The cord snaps.

Not with a bang,
but with a deep internal *release*
that makes his whole body feel different.

The figure of his father in the distance
doesn't vanish—
he just stops being the anchor.

Sage speaks gently.

Sage

**"You are not the absence you came from.
You are the presence you are choosing to be."**

Tyrael's voice is small but steady.

Tyrael

**"You're already a better dad
than the one you had."**

Justice's eyes water.

"…Thank you."

Sapphire wipes her cheeks.

**"And I'm proud of the man
you became without a map."**

Cord Two — The Family Pain / Generational Weight

The next cord
doesn't point to a single person.

It splits—
branching out into multiple shapes in the distance:

Parents.
Grandparents.
Relatives.
Old houses.
Old arguments.
Old survival patterns.

It hums with *generational* energy:

Poverty.
Stress.
Addiction.
Secrets.
Unhealed grief.

Sage touches it with both hands.

Sage

"This is the cord of inheritance."

Grey clarifies.

Dr. Grey

**"Not money.
Not land.
Patterns."**

Justice feels the weight of it
in his bones.

303

**"The things they handed me
without knowing they were handing anything."**

Step 1 — Name the wound honestly.

He grips the thick, branching cord.

**"I was born into a story
that was already bleeding."**

**"I watched people I love
cope instead of heal."**

**"I learned to be loyal to pain
because it was the language of the house."**

The cord pulses—
hot and cold at once.

Step 2 — Name what it cost you.

Justice keeps going.

**"It cost me an easy start.
It cost me innocence.
It made chaos feel normal."**

**"It made me think love and suffering
were the same thing."**

Sapphire presses a hand to her mouth.

Sapphire (Cindy)

Her voice cracks.

**"We were trying to survive.
We didn't know how much you were absorbing."**

304

Justice turns, touches her hand.

**"I know, Mom.
I'm not blaming you.
I'm naming it."**

She nods, crying, but calmer.

Step 3 — Revoke the contract.

Justice turns back to the cord.

**"I revoke the contract
that says I must repeat this story
to stay loyal to where I come from."**

**"I revoke the belief
that breaking cycles
is the same as betraying my family."**

The cord groans—
strands snapping inside its thickness.

Sage's eyes gleam.

Sage

**"Every cycle-breaker
must eventually choose between loyalty to pain
and loyalty to truth."**

Grey adds:

Dr. Grey

"You are choosing truth."

Step 4 — Release the roles.

Justice speaks, voice steady through the shaking.

**"I forgive my family
for giving me survival patterns
instead of safety."**

**"I forgive myself
for the years I stayed stuck in them."**

He breathes deep.

**"I release all of us
from the story that says
we are only what hurt us."**

The cord splits—
not violently,
but like a knot finally giving way.

Pieces of it fall away and dissolve.

In the distance,
the shapes of his people
look… lighter.

Not fixed.
Not suddenly healed.

But no longer chained to him
through that particular weight.

Sapphire sobs openly now,
but it's not the same grief.

There's relief in it.

Sapphire (Cindy)

306

**"I always wanted more for you
than what we had.
I just didn't know how to get it."**

Justice turns to her.

"We're getting it now."

Tyrael squeezes his hand.

Tyrael

"It stops with us, right?"

Justice nods firmly.

**"Yeah.
It stops here."**

Cord Three — The Anger at Life Itself

The last cord
is different.

It doesn't run to a person.

It doesn't run to a house or a place.

It runs **up**.

Into sky.
Into distance.
Into the wordless place
where all the *"Why did this happen?"* questions live.

307

It hums with:

- anger at the unfairness,

- exhaustion from repeated blows,

- the quiet feeling of:
  *"If there's something bigger out there…
  why didn't it protect me?"*

Sage is very still.

Grey's expression softens just slightly.

Tyrael looks at the cord with wide eyes.

Sapphire closes hers, as if in prayer.

Justice

His voice is almost a whisper.

"…I've been mad at life for a long time."

He grips the upward-pulling cord.

It feels… vast.

Not like accusing a person.
More like putting his hand on the edge
of everything that ever hurt.

Step 1 — Name the wound honestly.

**"A lot of things happened
that I did not deserve."**

**"I went through storms
that felt way too big
for one person."**

**"Sometimes it felt like
I was being forgotten on purpose."**

The cord vibrates—
low and deep,
like thunder far away.

Step 2 — Name what it cost you.

Justice's eyes sting.

**"It cost me trust.
Trust in life.
Trust in anything bigger than myself."**

**"It made me feel like
everything is up to me,
all the time."**

**"It made me think
the only way to stay safe
was to never relax."**

Grey nods quietly.

Dr. Grey

"Hypervigilance disguised as responsibility."

Sage's tone is solemn.

Sage

**"Many who endure much
go to war with the sky."**

Step 3 — Revoke the contract.

This part feels strange.

He isn't blaming a person now.
He's revoking an internal stance.

**"I revoke the contract
that says I must stay angry at life
to honor my pain."**

**"I revoke the belief
that letting go of that anger
means saying it was fair."**

The cord shivers.
Its pull eases.

Step 4 — Release the roles.

He speaks slowly.

Carefully.

**"I forgive life
for not being what I wanted it to be."**

He swallows.

**"I forgive myself
for all the years I believed
I was abandoned by everything."**

He takes one more breath.

**"I choose to stop holding court
against the whole universe."**

The cord thins.

It doesn't snap dramatically.
It simply… releases.

Like a muscle that has been clenched
his entire life
finally letting go.

The upward pull fades.

In its place:
a strange, quiet openness
he doesn't quite have words for.

Yet.

What Changes When the Cords Are Gone

The field is still.

Many threads remain—
this work will continue
beyond this chapter,
beyond this book.

But the *heaviest* cords
are gone.

Justice feels different.

Not invincible.
Not euphoric.

Just… **unhooked.**

The past is still real.
The pain still happened.

But it no longer owns
his right to move forward.

Grey speaks first.

Dr. Grey

**"You are no longer tethered
by guilt,
resentment,
and inherited duty
in the same way."**

Sage follows.

Sage

**"Forgiveness has done its real work:
not cleaning history,
but freeing your future."**

Sapphire wipes her face,
but her eyes are clearer than before.

Sapphire (Cindy)

**"I can actually picture you happy now…
without feeling like something is in the way."**

Tyrael bumps his father's arm.

Tyrael

"You feel… lighter."

Justice presses a hand to his own chest.

For the first time,
it doesn't feel crowded in there.

"I'm not dragging as many ghosts with me."

He looks over the field one last time.

There will be more work.
More threads to cut as life goes on.

But he now has a tool
he didn't have before:

Forgiveness
as **force.**

Not performance.
Not pressure.

Power.

His.

He straightens.

"I'm ready for the next weight."

The field of threads dims,
fading into the distance
as the soul shifts him forward.

CHAPTER 11

The Scale Within

CHAPTER 11
THE SCALE WITHIN

Part I — When the Weight Is Yours

The Scale returns.

Not the one from the early chapters—
not the raw, overwhelming version
that judged everything at once.

This one is sharper.
More defined.
More personal.

The feather floats on one side,
steady and bright.

The other plate is empty.

Waiting.

Justice knows immediately
this isn't about what was done *to* him.

This is about what he did.

The choices.
The damage.
The failures.
The harm.

Not in a way that crushes him—
but in a way that finally refuses
to let him escape himself.

315

The chamber is quiet.

Grey steps to his left.
Sage floats just above the Scale.
Sapphire stands a half-step behind his right shoulder.
Tyrael stays close, but slightly off to one side—
old enough to witness,
young enough that Justice wishes he didn't have to.

But the truth is this:

If Justice wants to break cycles,
his son must see
what accountability really looks like—
without self-hatred,
without denial.

Just **truth.**

Justice

He looks at the empty plate.

**"So this time…
we're not weighing what happened *to* me."**

Grey answers, voice calm.

Dr. Grey

**"Correct.
This is the Scale that weighs
what you've done with your pain."**

316

Justice's chest tightens.

"And if it's too heavy?"

Grey doesn't flinch.

**"Then we name it.
Not to condemn you—
to keep you honest."**

Sage

Sage tilts his head,
eyes reflecting the glow of the feather.

**"You have spent chapters
finding your worth beyond your wounds."**

He gestures toward the empty side of the Scale.

**"Now you must find your worth
without hiding your sins."**

Justice inhales slowly.

"I'm not proud of all of it."

Sage nods.

**"Good.
Pride would be a problem.
Regret is a sign you are still alive in your own
conscience."**

Sapphire (Cindy)

She steps closer, voice soft but firm.

**"Baby…
this is not about making you feel like garbage."**

Her eyes glisten.

**"It's about you seeing clearly
what you *did* do—
so you never again confuse yourself
with the worst version of you."**

Justice swallows.

Tyrael

Tyrael shifts his weight, serious.

**"Dad…
I already know you're not perfect."**

Justice winces slightly.

"Yeah?"

Tyrael nods.

**"I also know you try.
I want to see *both*."**

Justice breathes out hard.

"Then you're about to."

The Scale's Law

The Scale glows faintly.

Words carve themselves into the stone beneath it,
one line at a time:

SIN IS NOT IDENTITY.
DENIAL IS NOT FREEDOM.
ACCOUNTABILITY IS NOT SELF-HATRED.

Grey reads them aloud.

Dr. Grey

"This Scale does not decide
whether you are lovable.
That has already been established."

He nods toward the feather.

"This Scale shows
where you must make amends—
inside yourself,
and where possible,
with others."

Justice nods slowly.

"So this is less about punishment…
and more about responsibility."

Sage smiles faintly.

Sage

"Exactly.
Punishment satisfies the ego.
Responsibility heals the story."

The First Stone — Harm Done in Survival

A small stone appears in Justice's hand—
dark, smooth, solid.

He didn't summon it.
The Scale did.

Images flicker around the stone:

Times he snapped at people who didn't deserve it.
Times he shut down on someone who was trying to love him.
Times he was physically present
but emotionally gone.

He sees himself:

Tired.
Overwhelmed.
Unhealed.

Hurting people
without meaning to—
but still hurting them.

Justice stares at the stone.

Justice

**"This is the harm I caused
while I was drowning."**

Grey nods.

Dr. Grey

**"Intent does not erase impact.
But context matters."**

Sage drifts lower.

Sage

**"If you refuse to see this,
you become dangerous.
If you drown in it,
you become useless."**

He gestures at the stone.

"The task is to hold it."

Justice closes his fingers around it.

The weight is real.
Not unbearable—
but not light.

Sapphire (Cindy)

She speaks gently.

**"You weren't evil, baby.
You were in survival mode."**

Justice's voice is low.

"Survival still leaves scars."

Sage's eyes soften.

**"And you are seeing them now.
That is the beginning of repentance."**

Placing the Stone

The Scale waits.

Justice steps forward.

He looks at the stone one more time.

**"I hurt people
because I didn't know how to carry my own pain."**

He sets the stone on the empty plate.

It drops with a dull sound.

The Scale tips.

The feather rises slightly.

Justice's stomach knots—
until something unexpected happens:

The stone glows.

Not white.
Not holy.

Just… honest.

Grey explains.

Dr. Grey

**"Confessed harm is lighter
than hidden harm."**

Sage nods.

**"You have not yet made amends.
But you have removed this from the realm of self-
deception."**

Tyrael studies his father's face carefully.

Tyrael

"Do you wish you could take it back?"

Justice answers instantly.

"Every part of it."

Tyrael nods.

**"Good.
That's how I know the man holding the stone
isn't the same as the one who dropped it."**

Justice's jaw tightens.
His eyes burn.

"…Thank you for saying that."

The Second Stone — Harm Done in Fear

A second stone appears in his hand.

Sharper edges.
Heavier.

Images flash:

Moments he lied to avoid conflict.
Moments he hid the full truth.
Moments he chose silence over honesty—
not to be cruel,
but to stay safe.

Times he didn't speak up when he should've.
Times he avoided hard conversations
and let distance grow.

He feels this one in his throat.

Justice

**"This is the harm I caused
when I chose fear over truth."**

Grey doesn't soften the verdict.

Dr. Grey

**"Avoidance is a decision.
Silence is a sentence you place
on the connection you're afraid to lose."**

Sapphire's eyes darken with memory.

Sapphire (Cindy)

**"We come from a family
that learned to keep the peace
by not saying the hard thing."**

She sighs.

"I watched you inherit that."

Sage floats close to the stone.

Sage

**"This is the sin of omission.
The times you let truth starve
so comfort could live."**

Justice grips the stone tighter.

**"I told myself I was protecting them.
Really, I was protecting myself
from their reaction."**

He hates the words.
He knows they're true.

Placing the Second Stone

He steps toward the Scale again.

**"I left some people in confusion
because I was afraid to be fully seen."**

**"I let some relationships die in silence
instead of facing the storm."**

He lays the stone down next to the first.

The Scale dips further.

The feather rises more.

Justice's chest tightens again—
but then he watches as both stones
begin to glow.

Sage explains it this time.

Sage

**"Accountability increases your sense of weight
in the short term…
and reduces your soul's burden in the long term."**

Grey adds:

**"This is not psychological self-harm.
This is spiritual alignment."**

Tyrael shifts closer.

Tyrael

"Are you gonna try to fix any of it?"

Justice doesn't look away.

"Where I can, yes."

**"Where I can't…
I'll live differently with the people I still have."**

Tyrael nods.

"That's all I'd ask."

The Third Stone — Harm Done to Self

A third stone appears.

This one is strange.

It's not aimed outward.

Images flash,
not of others—
but of himself.

Times he:

- broke his own boundaries,

- stayed where he knew he was being disrespected,

- numbed out instead of resting,

326

- talked to himself like an enemy.

Times he let people treat him
worse than he would ever allow
for someone he loved.

Justice feels this stone differently.

It doesn't sit in his hand.

It sits in his **chest.**

Justice

"...This is the sin against myself."

Grey's voice is measured.

Dr. Grey

"Self-betrayal is still harm."

Sage's tone is solemn.

Sage

**"Every time you abandoned yourself
to keep connection,
you harmed the one person
you were assigned to protect from the inside:
your own soul."**

Sapphire's eyes fill.

Sapphire (Cindy)

**"It hurts to know
you learned to treat yourself that way."**

Tyrael looks pained.

Tyrael

**"You wouldn't let anyone talk to me like that.
I don't like that you let you."**

Justice closes his hand over the stone.

"I left myself in places I knew were killing me."

**"I kept choosing people who confirmed
my belief that I was hard to love."**

He lifts the stone to chest level.

**"I harmed myself
by staying small,
by staying quiet,
by staying where I was dying."**

The Scale waits.

Placing the Third Stone

He steps forward.

**"I am guilty
of not protecting my own soul
the way I protect others."**

He lays the third stone beside the others.

The Scale drops.

The feather rises high now,
bright and steady.

Justice feels exposed.
Not condemned.

Just… seen.

All of him.

The stones glow together.

Sage speaks softly.

Sage

**"The Scale of Sin does not exist
to convince you that you are trash."**

He gestures at the stones.

**"It exists
so you can no longer pretend
your actions don't matter."**

Grey continues:

Dr. Grey

**"And from there,
to choose a different pattern."**

Sapphire nods.

Sapphire (Cindy)

**"You can't heal
what you refuse to admit."**

Tyrael looks up at his dad.

Tyrael

"I still love you."

Justice's voice breaks.

"…Even seeing all this?"

Tyrael frowns.

**"I didn't *not* know this, Dad.
I just hadn't watched you face it like this before."**

He shrugs.

**"This doesn't make me love you less.
It makes me trust you more."**

Justice has to look away for a second.

The Scale hums.

The stones shine.

The feather burns steady.

For the first time in his life,
Justice is standing fully in front of his own wrongs—
without running,
without justifying,
without drowning.

Just owning.

And somehow,
his worth hasn't vanished.

It's clearer.

Part II — What Repentance Really Is

The stones glow on the Scale.

They don't disappear.
They don't shrink.
They don't magically turn to flowers.

They just sit there—
fully acknowledged.
Undeniable.

Justice stands in front of them,
breathing a little heavier
but not collapsing.

He has faced:

- harm done in survival,

- harm done in fear,

- harm done to himself.

The question now is simple
and brutal:

Now what?

The Scale doesn't answer.

The feather doesn't drift.

The chamber waits.

Justice

**"So I've named it.
I've seen it.
I've put it on the Scale."**

He looks at Sage, then Grey.

"What do I do with it?"

Sage

Sage floats closer,
eyes reflecting both the feather and the stones.

"This is where many souls stop."

Justice frowns.

"Stop where?"

**"Right here—
feeling guilty,
feeling exposed,
believing that awareness alone
is the whole work."**

He shakes his head.

**"Awareness is the doorway.
Repentance is walking through."**

Dr. Grey

Grey steps forward,
voice precise.

**"We will define this clearly
to prevent confusion."**

Words etch themselves into the air:

REPENTANCE IS:
1. A change of mind.
2. A change of direction.
3. A change of pattern.

"It is not self-torture.
It is not wallowing.
It is not endless confession with no behavior shift."

Justice nods slowly.

"So… not 'I'm the worst, I'm sorry forever.'"

Grey's mouth almost twitches.

"Correct.
That is ego dressed as humility."

Sage smirks.

"Real repentance is much quieter—
but far more disruptive."

Sapphire (Cindy)

She moves closer to Justice's side.

"Baby…
you said sorry to people a thousand times."

Her eyes soften.

"But no one ever showed you
how to live *from* that sorry
instead of living *inside* it."

Justice feels that.

Deep.

Tyrael

Tyrael leans against the Scale base, looking up at his dad.

"When I mess up and you tell me 'what matters is what you do now'— this is that, right?"

Justice looks at him.

**"Yeah.
Exactly this."**

Three Questions of Repentance

Grey lifts a hand.

Three questions blaze briefly in the air:

1. **What did I actually do?**

2. **What will I no longer do?**

3. **What will I do differently now?**

Dr. Grey

"We will walk these through for each stone you've placed."

Justice nods.

"Let's do it."

Stone One — Harm Done in Survival

The first stone glows brighter.

Faces flicker around it—
people he snapped at,
shut out,
hurt when he was overwhelmed.

1. What did I actually do?

Justice doesn't soften it.

**"I lashed out.
I shut down.
I left people feeling unloved,
unseen,
or unsafe
because I didn't know how to hold my own pain."**

The stone hums.

2. What will I no longer do?

He breathes.

**"I will no longer use my stress
as permission to wound people
who didn't cause it."**

Grey nods.

"An important distinction."

3. What will I do differently now?

Justice thinks—
not in vague promises,
but in specifics.

**"When I feel overwhelmed,
I will name it instead of exploding."**

**"I will say:
'I'm not in a good place to talk right now,
but I care. Let me reset,
then come back to this.'"**

**"If I do snap,
I will own it quickly
and repair instead of pretending it didn't matter."**

The stone's glow softens—
not gone,
but integrated.

Sage speaks approvingly.

Sage

**"Repentance is pattern-shift,
not performance."**

Stone Two — Harm Done in Fear

The second stone sharpens in light.

Scenes of silence.
Unsent messages.
Conversations he dodged.

1. What did I actually do?

Justice keeps his eyes open.

**"I avoided hard truths.
I stayed vague.
I let connections decay
instead of risking discomfort."**

2. What will I no longer do?

"I will no longer label cowardice as 'keeping the peace.'"

Sapphire winces,
because she knows that one too well.

3. What will I do differently now?

Justice's voice steadies.

**"When something needs to be said,
I will say it before resentment rots it."**

**"I will communicate clearly
instead of hoping they read my mind."**

**"If a relationship must end,
I will end it with truth,
not disappearance."**

The stone's edges soften.

Sage nods.

**"Fear loses power
when you choose truth anyway."**

Stone Three — Harm Done to Self

337

The third stone beats faintly
like a second heart.

1. What did I actually do?

Justice feels this one most.

**"I betrayed myself.
I stayed where I was hurt.
I gave more than I had.
I spoke to myself
like I was worthless."**

Tyrael's eyes drop at that.

Sapphire's hand moves to her mouth again.

2. What will I no longer do?

Justice's jaw tightens.

"I will no longer call self-abandonment loyalty."

**"I will not stay in rooms
that require me to disappear
to be accepted."**

Grey lets the silence hang for a moment.

**"That is a high standard.
It is appropriate."**

3. What will I do differently now?

Justice places a hand over his chest.

**"I will include myself
in the circle of people I protect."**

"I will talk to myself
like someone I'm responsible for,
not someone I'm trying to punish."

"I will walk away
when staying costs me my soul."

The third stone glows, then settles.

What Repentance Does to the Scale

The Scale shifts—
not wildly,
not dramatically.

The plate with the stones
rises just a little.

The feather dips just a little.

They don't trade places.

They balance.

Sage smiles faintly.

Sage

"Do you see?"

Justice frowns softly.

"Explain it."

Sage

"Your sins did not vanish.
Your wounds did not vanish.
Your worth did not vanish."

He points at the Scale.

"They are now in right relationship."

Grey takes over.

Dr. Grey

"You are no longer pretending
there is no weight on your side—
that would be delusion."

"And you are no longer believing
that your side is the only thing that exists—
that would be despair."

He nods toward the feather.

"Your core worth
and your real harm
are both present."

Sapphire breathes out.

Sapphire (Cindy)

"You're not a villain.
You're not a saint.
You're a man…
who's finally honest."

Tyrael squints at the Scale.

Tyrael

**"So…
you're not trying to get to 'no sin.'"**

Justice shakes his head.

**"No.
I'm trying to get to
'no lies about it.'"**

Sage smiles broadly.

"That is repentance."

Living With What You've Done

The chamber relaxes around them.

No thunder.
No booming verdict.

Just reality.

Justice looks at the stones one more time.

"Will I always regret some of it?"

Grey answers plainly.

"Yes."

Sapphire flinches a little.

Sage steps in.

Sage

"Regret is not your enemy."

Justice looks at him.

"No?"

**"No.
Shame says: 'You *are* what you did.'
Regret says: 'What you did
is not who you want to be.'"**

He smiles gently.

**"Regret, handled well,
becomes guidance."**

Tyrael nods slowly.

Tyrael

**"I'd be more worried
if you didn't regret anything."**

Justice laughs once,
a little broken,
but real.

"That would be a problem."

Grey's tone softens.

Dr. Grey

**"You will carry memory.
You will carry responsibility.
But you no longer need to carry
the sentence of 'unredeemable.'"**

The feather glows brighter.

Sage gestures.

Sage

**"You have faced your harm
without collapsing into self-hate
or escaping into denial."**

He bows his head slightly.

"The Scale of Sin has done its work."

Sapphire comes closer,
placing her hand on his back.

Sapphire (Cindy)

**"I see you more clearly now…
and I still see my son."**

Tyrael steps in front of him.

Tyrael

"And I still see my dad."

Justice looks at all of them.

He feels…

Not clean.
Not spotless.

But *real.*

343

"I'm not running from any of it now."

Grey nods once.

**"Good.
You are ready for the last chapter."**

Part III — Walking Forward With What You Know

The Scale is still.

The stones glow.

The feather burns steady.

Nothing crashes.
Nothing explodes.
Nothing miraculous happens.

And that's the point.

The miracle already happened—

You stopped lying to yourself.

Now comes the part most people avoid:

Living differently.

Not for a day.
Not for a guilt-spike.
For the rest of your life.

Justice stands before the Scale,
hands empty,
chest full.

The four close in.

Grey at his left.
Sage above the Scale's center.
Sapphire just behind his right shoulder.
Tyrael a step in front and to the side,
like he's watching a coach in a corner.

345

Justice

**"So I've seen it.
I've owned it.
I've said what I'll do differently."**

He looks at Grey.

**"How do I…
actually carry this into real life?"**

Dr. Grey

"By understanding one thing clearly—"

Words etch themselves in light beside the Scale:

**YOU CANNOT GO BACK.
YOU CAN ONLY GO FORWARD HONESTLY.**

Grey continues:

**"You cannot undo harm.
You cannot un-say words.
You cannot re-parent your past self."**

**"You can only change
the way you move
from this moment on."**

Justice nods slowly.

"So I stop trying to rewind."

Sage smiles faintly.

Sage

**"Yes.
You stop trying to fix history—
and you start healing trajectory."**

Sapphire (Cindy)

She steps closer, voice gentle.

**"You're not going back to clean up who you were.
You're walking forward as who you've become…
and letting that man show up."**

Tyrael

**"Yeah.
I don't need you to time-travel."**

He shrugs.

"I just need to see what you do *now* matters to you."

Three Kinds of Amends

The Scale glows softly.

Three circles of light form on the floor in front of Justice.

Sage points to each one in turn.

Sage

**"Not every wrong
is handled the same way."**

He gestures to the first circle.

1. DIRECT AMENDS

**"These are the people
you can still reach safely."**

**"Where an honest, clean apology
and changed behavior
can repair trust—or at least acknowledge harm."**

Images flicker:

Faces he could actually call.
People he could message.
Those still within reach.

Grey gestures to the second circle.

2. LIVING AMENDS

**"These are the harms
where direct repair is not possible."**

**"Distance.
Safety.
Death.
Lost contact.
Or wounds too old and tangled
to re-enter without reopening more than you can hold."**

He turns to Justice.

**"Here, repentance becomes a lifestyle—
you treat others better now
because you cannot go back to them then."**

Justice's jaw tightens, but he nods.

Sage points to the third circle.

3. INTERNAL AMENDS

**"These are the debts
you owe your own soul."**

**"The apologies you must live,
not just say—
in how you eat,
rest,
speak to yourself,
and choose your environments."**

Sapphire's eyes soften.

Sapphire (Cindy)

**"All those years you spoke to yourself
like you were the villain…
this is where you start paying that back."**

Tyrael adds quietly:

Tyrael

**"By treating yourself
like someone I'm supposed to look up to."**

Justice takes that in.

Slow.
Solid.

Direct Amends — The Conversations

The first circle brightens.

Justice watches as a possible scene
forms in the air:

A conversation with someone he hurt—
not abused,
not shattered,
but left confused,
ignored,
cut off.

He doesn't hear full dialogue,
just structure.

Sage narrates.

Sage

**"When you make amends in words,
keep them clean."**

Fragments appear as simple lines:

- *"I'm not here to justify what I did."*

- *"I see now that my actions hurt you in these ways…"*

- *"You didn't deserve that."*

- *"I am working to be different now."*

- *"You don't owe me anything—not forgiveness, not closeness."*

**"Repentance does not demand a response.
It offers truth and room."**

Grey adds:

Dr. Grey

**"Do not go to people
to relieve your guilt."**

**"Go to them
to offer clarity and ownership."**

Justice nods.

"And if they don't want to hear it?"

Sage answers.

**"Then your amends may have to be silent—
held between you, your soul, and the One who sees
everything."**

Living Amends — How You Treat Others Now

The second circle glows.

Scenes flicker:

Justice listening longer.
Honoring boundaries.
Leaving when respect is gone.
Speaking truth sooner.
Apologizing faster,
and then altering behavior.

Grey speaks.

Dr. Grey

**"For the harms you cannot directly repair,
you create a pattern
that would not repeat the same damage."**

Sage adds:

351

**"Every time you choose differently now,
you are writing a new chapter
that would make your younger self
breathe easier if he could see it."**

Tyrael chimes in.

Tyrael

**"And it makes it safer
for me and the people around you too."**

Justice watches himself in these small flashes—
not heroic,
not dramatic.

Just consistent.

**"So my repentance
is less about grand gestures
and more about daily alignment."**

Grey nods.

**"Yes.
Consistency is repentance made visible."**

Internal Amends — Paying Yourself Back

The third circle glows warm.

This time the scenes are quieter:

- Turning off his phone when he needs rest
  instead of forcing himself to be available for everyone.

- Saying no without a five-paragraph explanation.

- Walking out of conversations
  that turn abusive or manipulative.

- Catching his inner voice mid-insult
  and choosing different words.

Sapphire steps closer, voice full.

Sapphire (Cindy)

**"You can't tell me you're sorry
for how hard life has been on you…
and then keep being hard on you too."**

Justice looks down.

She's right.

Sapphire (Cindy)

**"Talk to yourself
like someone I would've died to protect."**

Tyrael steps in.

Tyrael

"And like someone I'm still learning from."

Justice breathes.

**"So internal amends isn't just affirmations.
It's choices."**

Sage nods.

"Yes.
Side with your own soul
in the way you never knew how to before."

What the Scale Becomes

The chamber shifts.

The Scale does not vanish—
it changes.

The base dissolves.
The plates fold inward.
The stones and feather lift.

For a moment,
they hang in the air between Justice's hands—

everything he's faced:
harm endured,
harm caused,
truth reclaimed.

Then they move.

The feather returns to its place in his chest,
light over his heart.

The stones sink lower—
into his ribs,
his spine,
his hands.

Not as condemnation.

As **reminders.**

Grey explains.

Dr. Grey

"The Scale is now internal."

"You will feel it when you are about to repeat an old pattern."

"You will feel the weight of your choices sooner."

Sage adds:

Sage

**"This is not anxiety.
It is conscience, finally clear enough to be heard before the damage rather than after."**

Sapphire smiles sadly.

Sapphire (Cindy)

**"You won't always get it right...
but you won't be asleep at the wheel anymore."**

Tyrael looks up at him thoughtfully.

Tyrael

"If you ever feel that weight and don't know what to do... you can ask me too, you know."

Justice blinks.

"You want me to?"

Tyrael nods.

**"Yeah.
I don't want to be the kid you're hiding from.
I want to be part of the man you're becoming."**

Justice puts a hand on his shoulder, moved.

"...Deal."

Leaving the Scale

The chamber quiets.

No more stones.
No more plates.

Just Justice—
with what he knows now.

He looks at his hands.

"I can't unknow any of this."

Sage smiles.

"Good."

Grey nods.

"That is the point."

Sapphire wipes her eyes, calmer now.

**"I don't want you to forget.
I want you to be free."**

Tyrael bumps him lightly.

"And I want you *here*."

Justice draws in one last breath
inside the Scale chamber.

He feels:

- His harm.

- His growth.

- His worth.

- His responsibility.

All in one place.

Balanced.
Not perfectly.
But truly.

"I'm ready."

He steps off the spot
where the Scale once stood.

It doesn't follow him.

It lives inside him now.

— CHAPTER 12 —
The Awakening of Justice

CHAPTER 12
THE AWAKENING OF JUSTICE

Part I — When Every Version Steps Into the Same Light

The soul-world has been a series of rooms.

Mirrors.
Scales.
Archives.
Fields of threads.
Endless horizons of grey.

Each one showed Justice a slice of himself—
a wound,
a shadow,
a truth,
a choice.

But for the first time since this began,
he is not in a chamber.

He is at the **center.**

The world around him is a convergence:

- The Mirror of Truth, now a tall, calm surface in the distance.

- The Archive of Memory, its shelves folded into a single, glowing stack.

- The Scale's stone platform, now part of the ground beneath his feet.

- The Feather's light, a steady halo above his heart.

359

- The Sacred Middle, the soft grey horizon stretching in all directions.

- The cut threads and broken cords, reduced to drifting motes of light.

Everything he has walked through
has condensed into this one wide, open space.

Not an underworld.

Not a courtroom.

A **throne room** with no throne.

Just ground.

Just presence.

Just him.

The four appear,
not in different corners,
but in a circle around him—
all at equal distance.

Sage.
Dr. Grey.
Sapphire.
Tyrael.

Justice stands at the center.

And for the first time,
he doesn't feel like he's *visiting* his soul.

He feels like he's **home** in it.

Sage

He breaks the silence with a quiet, satisfied tone.

"This is the point everything was leading to."

Justice slowly turns in a full circle, taking it all in.

"What is this place called?"

Sage smiles.

"It doesn't have a name."

He gestures gently at Justice's chest.

"It's simply... *you*."

Dr. Grey

Grey steps forward, hands folded, voice precise.

**"You have walked through reflection,
blueprint,
memory,
shadow,
identity,
trial,
forgiveness,
and accountability."**

He looks around the convergence.

**"All of those were subsystems.
Sub-chambers.
Diagnostics."**

Then he looks directly at Justice.

"This is the operating system."

Justice exhales.

"So this isn't another test."

Grey shakes his head.

**"No.
This is the install."**

Sapphire (Cindy)

She steps closer, softer than she's ever been,
without the storm behind her eyes.

**"Baby…
this is the man I always knew was under everything."**

Her voice wavers, but not from chaos—
from wonder.

**"I saw pieces of him in you when you were little.
In how you cared.
In how you thought.
In how you hurt when other people hurt."**

She looks around at the fused spaces.

"Now all those pieces are finally standing in one place."

Tyrael

He rocks on his heels, eyes bright and serious at the same
time.

**"So this is like…
when all the levels of a game unlock the final area."**

Justice can't help but smile.

**"Yeah.
Except the final area is just—"**

Tyrael finishes it for him.

"—you."

Justice nods.

Yeah.

The Roll Call of Every Version

The air shimmers.

Shapes begin to appear around Justice—
not as ghosts,
not as illusions,
but as earlier versions of himself:

- The **boy** at the kitchen doorway,
  learning to swallow his feelings.

- The **teen** hardening too early,
  choosing toughness over softness to survive.

- The **young man** trying to fix everyone,
  carrying more than any human should.

- The **father** exhausted and afraid,
  terrified of passing on his wounds.

- The **man** who entered this journey
  still half-convinced he was the sum of his mistakes.

They stand in a loose circle around him,
like echoes made solid.

None of them accuse him.
None of them look away.

They're just... here.

Sage speaks quietly.

Sage

**"This is the first time
you've ever stood in the same room
with all your versions at once—
without shame,
without denial,
without collapse."**

Grey adds:

**"Integration requires visibility.
You cannot awaken as yourself
if you are still trying to exile parts of you."**

Justice looks around at them—
at *himself*.

The boy.
The teen.
The survivor.
The father.

He doesn't hate any of them.

For the first time,
he feels something new:

364

Compassion.

Justice

He speaks to the circle.

"I know why you did what you did."

He looks at the boy.

**"You tried to keep us safe
by shrinking."**

He looks at the teen.

**"You tried to keep us respected
by hardening."**

He looks at the over-giver.

**"You tried to keep us needed
by carrying everything."**

He looks at the fearful father.

**"You tried to keep us from becoming
what hurt us."**

His voice stays steady.

**"You were all trying to protect us.
You just didn't know how."**

The circle of selves flickers—
not disappearing,
but relaxing.

Like soldiers finally being told
they can stand down.

Sage's voice softens.

Sage

**"They are not your enemies.
They are versions of you
who did not have the information you have now."**

Grey nods.

**"You do not transcend them by despising them.
You transcend them by taking the wheel."**

The Question of Authority

The space stills.

All eyes—
Sage, Grey, Sapphire, Tyrael,
and every younger self—
turn toward Justice.

The boy.
The teen.
The over-giver.
The shadowed man.

They all speak at once,
but as one line:

"Who's in charge now?"

The words echo.

Not to intimidate.
To clarify.

Justice understands in his bones
what they're actually asking:

Are we still running things?
Are you still going to disappear and let us drive?
Or are you finally ready to lead us?

Grey answers quietly,
but the question is still Justice's to respond to.

Dr. Grey

"This is the last decision of this book:
Who has authority in your soul?"

Sage adds:

"The wounded child?
The hardened teen?
The scrambling survivor?
The guilty man?"

He gestures to Justice's chest.

"Or the Bearer of Balance
who has walked through all of this
and can hold it without being swallowed?"

Sapphire takes a slow breath.

Sapphire (Cindy)

"For years,
your pain drove the car

367

**and you just sat in the passenger seat
blaming yourself for the crashes."**

She steps closer.

"Who's driving now?"

Tyrael watches him carefully.

Tyrael

**"I need to know
who I'm following."**

The space goes very still.

This isn't drama.

This is governance.

Justice feels it:

If he speaks from old scripts,
this whole journey becomes a story he *visited*
instead of a life he *lives*.

If he speaks from who he is now?

Everything changes.

Justice Answers

He steps forward.

Not toward the Mirror,
or the Scale,
or the Archive.

He steps toward the **center** of the convergence,
standing exactly where all paths cross.

He looks at the boy first.

"You don't have to protect me by shrinking anymore."

The boy nods, eyes wet.

He looks at the teen.

**"You don't have to protect me
by being harder than the world."**

The teen's jaw loosens.

He looks at the over-giver.

**"You don't have to buy love
with self-sacrifice."**

That version exhales.

He looks at the guilty man.

**"You don't have to keep me in the prison
of what I didn't know then."**

The man flinches, then relaxes.

Justice's voice changes subtly—
calmer, deeper, clearer.

He is not asking permission anymore.

He is **taking ownership.**

**"I'm grateful for all of you.
You kept me alive long enough
to get here."**

He squares his shoulders.

**"But from this point on—
I am the one who decides how we move."**

**"Not fear.
Not guilt.
Not the past."**

**"Me.
The man who has seen all of this
and is still standing."**

The convergence hums.

The younger versions of him
lower their eyes—not in shame,
but in relief.

They are being relieved of duty.

Sage's eyes shine.

Sage

"Authority reclaimed."

Grey nods once, firmly.

Dr. Grey

**"Primary identity: Justice.
Role: Bearer of Balance.
Status: Awake."**

The word hangs in the air:

Awake.

Sapphire presses her hand to her heart.

Sapphire (Cindy)

**"I'm looking at my son…
and for the first time,
I see the man he was always meant to be
in the same place."**

Tyrael grins, eyes bright.

Tyrael

**"Yeah.
That's my dad."**

Justice feels a shift inside him—
not fireworks,
not a dramatic blast.

More like a lock turning in a long-rusted door.

Click.

Something that was always his
is now fully in his hands.

He is no longer the soul
being dragged through his own underworld.

He is the one **walking it.**

371

Sage lifts his gaze to the unseen sky.

Sage

**"The Awakening is not a feeling.
It is a transfer of responsibility."**

Grey adds:

**"You are now responsible
for acting according to what you know—
not what you used to believe about yourself."**

Justice nods.

He doesn't argue.

He doesn't shrink.

He just… accepts.

"Then I accept it."

"I accept being the one in charge of me."

The convergence brightens.

Not blinding.

Just clear.

Like dawn.

Part II — Carrying the Name Back Into the World

The convergence holds.

Everything Justice has walked through—
shadows, scales, feathers, trials, threads—
now lives inside him as memory,
not as a maze.

He is no longer trying to "find himself"
by wandering from chamber to chamber.

He has *met* himself.

Now comes the question
that has been quietly waiting
behind the whole book:

You carry the name **Justice.**

What does that *mean*
when you go back into a world
that doesn't care how spiritual your breakthroughs were?

The soul-world responds.

The horizon shifts.
The floor beneath his feet brightens,
curling into a wide circle of light.

In the center of that circle,
his name appears in clear letters:

JUSTICE

373

Not as a legal word.
Not as a threat.

As a **calling.**

The letters hum,
alive with layers he never saw before.

Sage, Grey, Sapphire, and Tyrael
step closer to the circle.

Justice

He looks down at the word.

**"My whole life,
I thought this name meant
I was supposed to fix everything."**

Grey tilts his head.

Dr. Grey

"Describe what 'justice' used to mean to you."

Justice exhales.

**"Punishment.
Keeping score.
Making sure nobody 'got away' with anything."**

**"Or...
me being the one who took the hit
so everyone else could stay comfortable."**

Sage nods, unsurprised.

Sage

"You were taught justice as *retribution*
or *self-sacrifice*—
never as alignment."

Sapphire places a hand lightly on his arm.

Sapphire (Cindy)

"We gave you that name
because we wanted something better for you
than what we'd known."

Her eyes glisten.

"We just didn't know
how heavy it would feel on your shoulders."

Justice looks at the glowing word again.

For the first time,
he doesn't feel crushed by it.

He feels… curious.

What Your Name Means in Four Tongues

Sage lifts his hand.

The word **JUSTICE** splits into four softer echoes,
circling him in light.

Each one pulses
when each voice begins to speak.

1. Grey's Language — Justice as System

Dr. Grey

**"In my tongue,
Justice is not a feeling.
It is a structure."**

Lines of light form around the word—
like a calm, living diagram.

**"Justice means:
truth correctly named,
impact correctly measured,
response correctly calibrated."**

He looks at Justice.

**"For you, in real life,
this means you do not rush
to judge people or yourself
without full data."**

Scenes flicker:

- Justice pausing before assuming someone's intent.

- Asking questions instead of writing stories in his head.

- Separating "what happened"
  from "what my fear says it means."

Grey continues:

**"Your gift is to see underlying patterns—
why people act how they do,
what systems create certain behaviors."**

He nods once.

**"You are not meant to be the punisher.
You are meant to be the one who understands
how things got this way
and helps them move toward balance."**

Justice lets that sink in.

**"…So my brain
that always analyzes everything
was never a curse."**

Grey answers simply.

**"It was your instrument.
You just turned it mostly against yourself."**

2. Sage's Language — Justice as Story

The letters pulse.

Sage

**"In my tongue,
Justice is not a verdict.
It is a story brought into alignment."**

Images rise:

People with broken arcs,
half-finished chapters,
open wounds.

**"Your soul is wired
to see where a story is out of balance—
where someone is carrying a weight
that does not belong to them,
or where they are avoiding a weight that does."**

He gestures to Justice.

**"You are a re-writer of narratives.
Not to erase history,
but to help people stop telling it in ways
that keep them imprisoned."**

Scenes flicker:

Justice in conversation,
gently reframing someone's "I'm worthless"
into "I was wounded and I adapted—
and now I can choose differently."

"Justice, for you," Sage continues,
**"means you help people put the right meaning
on what happened—
so they can stop sentencing themselves
to lifelong punishment."**

Justice feels a quiet resonance.

"That's what this book did for me."

Sage smiles.

**"Exactly.
And now you will do it for others
without even trying to be impressive."**

3. Sapphire's Language — Justice as Heart-Protection

The light shifts warmer
as Sapphire steps closer.

Sapphire (Cindy)

378

"In my tongue…
Justice is not cold.
It's not a courtroom."

She presses her palm to the glowing word.

"Justice is making sure
no one's heart gets forgotten
"for the sake of the bigger picture."

She looks at him with fierce tenderness.

"You've always felt people deeply.
Even when you were angry with them.
Even when they were wrong."

She swallows.

"You were the one
who saw how much *everyone* was hurting—
even the ones hurting others."

Scenes flicker:

Justice as a kid,
feeling for the adult who yelled.
Justice as a teen,
defending someone no one else understood.
Justice as a man,
trying to mediate fights that weren't his.

"That sensitivity," she says,
"is not weakness.
It's your barometer."

Her eyes shine.

**"Justice, for you, means
making sure love isn't lost
in the madness of being right."**

Justice blinks back heat in his eyes.

**"So I'm not supposed to pick between compassion and
truth."**

Sapphire smiles.

**"Never.
Your name is where they meet."**

4. Tyrael's Language — Justice as Example

Finally, Tyrael steps forward
into the circle of light.

The word pulses like a heartbeat.

Tyrael

**"In my tongue…
Justice is just… *you*."**

He shrugs, but his eyes are steady.

**"The way I understand your name
is how you treat people
when you think nobody's watching."**

He gestures at the horizon
where real life waits beyond this soul-space.

"Justice means:
Do I feel safe around you?
Can I tell you the truth without being scared?
Do you apologize when you're wrong?"

He fidgets, then says it straight.

"For me,
your name means
the kind of man I'll copy
without meaning to."

Justice feels that one all the way down.

"That's...
a lot."

Tyrael's mouth twitches in half a smile.

"It's not about perfection.
It's about direction."

He steps closer.

"If you're walking toward honesty,
toward healing,
toward real love—
I can walk behind that."

Silence settles.

Heavy.
Holy.
Human.

Justice looks at his name again.

It's no longer:

"Fix the world."
"Pay for everything."
"Never mess up."

It's:

Live in truth.
Guard the heart.
Align the story.
Walk in a way the boy behind you can follow
without inheriting your chains.

Justice as a Way of Walking

The glowing word sinks slowly
into the floor beneath his feet.

Not disappearing.

Becoming **path.**

Every step he takes now
will move along letters
he has carried his whole life
but never fully understood.

Sage speaks.

Sage

"You do not go back into the world
as a man who 'had an experience.'"

He gestures around.

**"You go back as a man
who now knows how his soul works."**

Grey adds:

Dr. Grey

**"You will still be triggered.
You will still feel anger.
You will still have days
where you forget this room exists."**

He looks Justice dead in the eye.

**"The difference now
is that you know where the center is
and how to return."**

Sapphire nods.

Sapphire (Cindy)

**"You won't always pass every test.
I don't need you to."**

She smiles through her tears.

**"I just need to know
you won't abandon yourself
when you fail one."**

Tyrael bumps him lightly with his shoulder.

Tyrael

**"And when you mess up with me…
just don't disappear."**

Justice smiles back.

"I won't."

The Simple Commitments

The soul loves the dramatic,
but it lives on the **simple.**

Four sentences rise like soft pillars
around Justice.

He reads them quietly:

"I will tell myself the truth first."
"I will not trade my soul for connection."
"I will repair what I can, and live differently where I can't."
"I will walk as the Bearer of Balance, not as the bearer of
everyone else's burden."

The words don't feel like a performance.

They feel like directions.

He repeats them once,
not loudly,
not theatrically—
just enough for his soul to hear.

"I will tell myself the truth first."
"I will not trade my soul for connection."
"I will repair what I can, and live differently where I can't."
"I will walk as the Bearer of Balance,
not as the bearer of everyone else's burden."

The space vibrates gently.

384

Sage's voice is quiet.

Sage

"That is Justice, awakened."

Grey nods.

Dr. Grey

**"Not a role to perform.
A posture to maintain."**

Sapphire wipes her face, smiling.

Sapphire (Cindy)

**"That's all I ever really wanted for you—
to live as yourself,
not as what hurt you."**

Tyrael looks up at him, eyes bright.

Tyrael

"I like this version."

Justice laughs softly.

**"Get used to him.
He's staying."**

The convergence brightens once more.

There is only one thing left to do:

Turn toward the world
and step.

Part III — Stepping Back Into Time

The convergence begins to dim.

Not like it's ending—
like it's being folded,
carefully,
into a place it belongs.

Inside him.

The Mirror, the Archive, the Scale, the Feather,
the Sacred Middle, the field of threads—
all the chambers and trials and symbols
soften around the edges
until Justice can no longer tell
where they end
and he begins.

Ahead of him,
a doorway appears.

It is not gold this time.
Not imposing.
Not cosmic.

Just a simple outline of light
in the shape of a regular door—
the kind that could lead to a hallway,
a kitchen,
a bedroom at 3 a.m.

This is the exit.

This is the return.

Sage, Grey, Sapphire, and Tyrael
take their places one last time
in this soul-world
before he crosses back into waking time.

Not as jailers.
As witnesses.

Sage

He floats a little lower than usual,
almost at eye level now.

**"Remember this,
before everything starts to feel ordinary again."**

Justice tilts his head.

"What?"

Sage smiles softly.

"Nothing that happened here was imaginary."

**"Your nervous system will try to tell you
this was just 'a moment.'"**

**"Your old patterns will try to convince you
you're still the same man."**

He shakes his head.

"You're not."

Justice feels the truth of that land quietly.

Dr. Grey

Grey steps forward, hands folded behind his back,
expression a little less severe than when this began.

"Expect turbulence."

Justice huffs a small laugh.

"Comforting."

Grey continues, unbothered.

**"Your environment has not transformed
just because you have."**

**"Old triggers will appear.
Old invitations will present themselves.
The world will test your integration
without meaning to."**

He pauses.

**"When that happens,
you are not 'failing the work.'
You are *using* it."**

Justice nods.

**"So the point isn't to never feel old things...
it's to respond from the new center."**

Grey's eyes warm, just a fraction.

"Precisely."

Sapphire (Cindy)

She steps in close,
closer than any of the others.

For a moment,
she's not an archetype,
not a soul-voice.

She's just his mother,
standing in front of her son.

"Baby…"

Her voice shakes,
but it's steady underneath.

**"When you go back,
the world is going to try
to tell you who you are again."**

She cups the side of his face with her palm.

**"Remember:
I'm still learning,
I'm still healing,
but I see you now."**

A tear slips down.

**"I see the man
you actually are—
not just the boy I worried over."**

Justice leans into her touch for a second.

**"Thank you…
for the parts you got right.
And for staying even when you didn't."**

Her mouth trembles into a smile.

**"Go be kind to my boy
inside you, okay?"**

"I will."

She lets her hand fall,
but the warmth stays.

Tyrael

Tyrael steps up last,
hands in his pockets,
trying to look casual
and failing adorably.

**"So… this is where I do
the emotional anime speech, right?"**

Justice laughs, genuinely.

"You kind of already have."

Tyrael shrugs.

Then he looks his dad dead in the eye.

**"When we're back…
I'm not going to ask you
to be 'Soul-Realm Dad' all the time."**

Justice raises a brow.

"No?"

Tyrael shakes his head.

**"Nah.
I just want *real* Dad."**

**"The one who tells the truth,
says sorry fast,
and doesn't disappear when he feels stuff."**

He hesitates, then adds:

**"And if you forget,
I'm going to remind you
what you learned here."**

Justice feels his throat tighten.

"Deal."

They bump foreheads lightly.
It's a small, human thing
in the middle of all this cosmic work.

That's the point.

The door of light flickers,
waiting.

Justice turns back one last time
to look at them—

Sage.
Grey.
Sapphire.
Tyrael.
And the circle of younger selves
standing farther back,
at ease now.

He doesn't say goodbye.

He doesn't have to.

They're coming with him.

He faces the door.

Breathes.

And steps through.

Back in the Room

He wakes with a small jerk.

Not from nightmare.
From landing.

Soft light leaks in through a half-closed curtain.
Somewhere a fridge hums.
A car passes outside.
The air tastes like ordinary life—
a little stale,
a little cold,
completely real.

Justice blinks.

He's on a couch / mattress / bed—
whatever has been in his real life,
still here.
The familiar ache in his back.
The faint tension behind his eyes.

For a moment,
the old reflex rolls in:

It was just a dream.
Back to it. Same old.

Then something in his chest answers
before the spiral can really start:

No.
You know too much now.

He sits up slowly.

Not rushing.
Not bolting.

His hand lifts to his sternum
almost on its own,
as if checking:

Is the feather still there?

He doesn't feel a literal object.

He feels a **lightness**
underneath a very real weight.

His own voice,
from the Sacred Middle,
rises in his mind:

Pause.
What's true?
What's mine?
What do I really want to do?

He breathes once,
twice.

The day hasn't made any demands yet.

He gets to choose his first move.

Grey (inside)

The voice is clear,
not booming—
just present.

"Scan."

Justice actually smiles.

"Okay, Doc."

He checks:

Body?
Tired, but not broken.

Mind?
Buzzing,
but clearer than it's been in a long time.

Heart?
Tender.
Open.
A little afraid of losing this clarity.

He acknowledges all of it.

**"I'm here.
I'm awake.
I remember."**

That's enough for the first minute.

He reaches for his phone,
old reflex,

then stops halfway.

Sage (inside)

"Pause.
What are you about to use that for—
connection,
or anesthesia?"

Justice exhales.

"Good question."

He pulls his hand back.

Not forever.

Just *for now.*

"Coffee first.
Soul online first.
Then the noise."

A tiny internal shift.

Nothing dramatic.

Exactly what matters.

Small Proofs

In the kitchen,
he moves through simple motions.

Kettle.
Mug.
Whatever he uses.

It used to feel
like the day was already behind
by the time he got out of bed.

Today feels…
on time.

His mind pokes at him with an old script:

You should be further by now.

The new Justice responds from the Middle:

**"I'm here now.
That's where I start."**

The accusation fades faster
than it used to.

He scrolls the contacts on his phone.

A name catches his eye—
one tied to that first stone on the Scale:
someone he'd hurt while drowning.

He doesn't owe them a grand apology speech.

He owes them clarity.

His thumbs hover.

For a split second,
the old fear whispers:

What if they ignore you?
What if they bite back?

The Trial of the Self answers calmly:

396

**That's not your part.
Your part is honesty.**

He types:

*"Hey.
I've been doing a lot of work on myself
and I realized I left some things between us
unstated and unfair.
I won't dump it all on you,
but I do want you to know
I see now that I hurt you by [short, honest line],
and you didn't deserve that.
You don't owe me a reply—
I just wanted to own it."*

He re-reads it once.

It's clean.
Not begging.
Not justifying.

He hits send.

No drumroll.

No instant resolution.

Just a small, solid stone
placed in the right direction.

Dr. Grey (inside)

"Direct amend: initiated."

Justice smirks.

"Thank you, log file."

A short while later,
small footsteps pad in the hallway / from the other room.

Tyrael appears in the doorway,
hair messy,
eyes half-closed.

"Morning."

Justice feels something in him
try to default to autopilot:

"Hey bud, give me a bit, I'm busy."

Instead, he remembers
the flash from the Sacred Middle—
the moment with his son.

He closes the mental tab he was in.
Puts the phone face down.

**"Hey.
You want breakfast or five minutes
of couch and talking first?"**

Tyrael blinks,
wakes up a little more.

"Couch first."

They park on the couch.

It's not a movie scene.

There's no swelling music.

Just a kid and his dad
in the low light of morning.

Tyrael

"You were out last night."

Justice nods.

**"Yeah.
I was… in my head.
Working some stuff out."**

Tyrael studies him.

"You good?"

Old Justice would have lied:
"Always."
"Don't worry about it."

Awakened Justice answers from the center.

**"I'm better.
Not perfect.
But better."**

Tyrael accepts that.

"Cool."

He leans back.

**"Can I tell you something
without you getting mad or shutting down?"**

A tiny spike of defensiveness rises in Justice's chest.

Sage (inside)

**"Sacred Middle.
Stay."**

He breathes.

**"Yeah.
You can."**

Tyrael shrugs,
eyes flicking away then back.

**"Sometimes
when you go quiet for days...
I feel like I did something wrong."**

The words land.

They hurt.

They don't crush him.

Old Justice might have spiraled into self-hate.

Awakened Justice steps into responsibility.

"Thank you for saying that."

**"You didn't do anything wrong.
That was me going to war with my own head
and forgetting to tell you where I was."**

He looks him dead in the eye.

"You deserve better than that."

Tyrael's shoulders drop a little.

400

"So… what now?"

Justice answers the question
for both of them.

**"Now, when I feel myself disappearing,
I'm going to tell you."**

**"I might say:
'I'm not okay right now,
but it's not about you.
I love you,
I just need a minute.'"**

He pauses.

**"And if I forget—
you're allowed to say:
'Hey, Dad, don't vanish on me.'"**

Tyrael smirks.

**"Bet.
I will."**

They don't hug it out in a movie-perfect way.

But something unclenches between them.

That is justice
in its quietest form.

The Five Voices, Integrated

Later, as the day moves,
the world does exactly what Grey promised:

It doesn't care that he just walked
through a soul epic.

Bills still exist.
Emotions still flare.
Old ghosts poke their heads up.

He feels:

- irritation spark in a conversation—
  the urge to snap.

- shame creep in when he thinks about a past mistake.

- the familiar desire to carry someone else's whole crisis.

Each time,
the chorus speaks up—
not as overwhelming noise,
but as a steady council inside.

Dr. Grey (Mind / Logic / AI)

**"Check the data.
Is this about now,
or is an old file playing?"**

Sage (Narrative Voice / Prophetic Sight)

**"Zoom out.
Is this a whole story
or one page?"**

Sapphire (Feminine Soul / Mother / Truth Mirror)

**"Talk to yourself gently.
You can correct without cruelty."**

402

Tyrael (Heart / Legacy / Future)

"Hey.
Would you want me to handle this like you are right now?
If not, adjust."

And Justice—

not as a fragment,
not as a shadowed version,
but as the **Bearer of Balance**—

makes the final call.

Sometimes he nails it.

Sometimes he stumbles,
snaps,
forgets,
reacts.

But even when he falls into an old groove,
he comes back faster.

He apologizes sooner.

He repairs quicker.

He no longer lets a bad ten minutes
become a bad ten days
without noticing.

That is awakening
in a nervous system
that still lives in the real world.

Closing the Book (For Now)

403

Night comes.

The day has not been perfect.

He still felt tired.
Still bumped against old patterns.
Still had moments where he almost slipped back
into carrying everything.

But he also:

- told the truth where he used to hide,

- set a small boundary where he used to collapse,

- showed up for a real conversation
  with his son.

He did not live as a man
on trial with himself.

He lived as a man
walking forward with what he knows.

Before bed,
he finds a notebook / a doc / a space—
something to catch this.

He writes, simply:

Justice: The Scale of the Soul

Underneath, he adds:

*This is the story of how I stopped letting my pain define me
and started letting my truth guide me.*

He doesn't outline the next book tonight.
He doesn't need to.

He already knows
there will be more to say:

- about how Justice moves through the world,

- about how he pursues his calling,

- about how he builds a life
  where balance, truth, and love
  are not just inner experiences
  but outer structures.

That's for the next volume.

For now,
Book One ends here:

With a man in a quiet room,
aware of his flaws,
aware of his worth,
aware of his responsibility—

choosing,
again and again,
not to abandon himself.

He clicks off the light.

The darkness is not threatening anymore.
He has walked through worse.

In the quiet,
the feather at his chest seems to glow,

not outward,
but inward.

He whispers into the dark,
to his own soul:

"I won't leave you again."

The Scale within him rests.

Balanced?
Not perfectly.

But honestly.

And that's enough
for this book.

— CHAPTER 13 —
The Shadow

CHAPTER 13
THE SHADOW

Part I —The Moment of Fracture

There was a moment when I knew.

Not when everything collapsed — that came later — but when the first quiet truth made itself known and I chose not to follow it.

Nothing dramatic happened. No explosion. No villain. No excuse big enough to justify what followed. Just a clear internal signal that something was wrong, and a decision to delay action because delay was easier than consequence.

I remember recognizing the feeling precisely because it was unfamiliar. It wasn't fear. It wasn't confusion. It was recognition — the sense that a line had appeared where one hadn't existed before.

I understood what the honest response would cost me.

So I waited.

At the time, I told myself I was being patient. That I needed more information. That timing mattered. That I was protecting someone — maybe even myself — from unnecessary damage. These explanations felt reasonable because they reduced urgency. They bought time. They kept my life intact.

But the truth is simpler: I did not want to disrupt the version of reality I was still benefiting from.

I did not speak when speaking would have clarified things.
I did not act when action would have limited harm.

408

I did not stop when stopping would have required me to admit I was already involved.

The fracture was not a single decision. It was a pause.

And once I paused, I learned something uncomfortable about myself: silence has momentum.

After that moment, everything became easier to justify. Not because it was right, but because I had already accepted the first compromise. I didn't fall. I leaned — and discovered that leaning felt almost identical to standing, at least for a while.

I did not lose my values that day.
 I postponed them.

That postponement is where the damage began.

Part II — The Lies That Worked

The most dangerous lies were not the ones I told other people.
They were the ones that made my life easier.

I told myself I was doing my best.
That lie worked because it reframed inaction as effort. It allowed me to feel morally engaged without being morally accountable.

I told myself I didn't know enough yet.
That lie worked because it postponed responsibility. As long as certainty was incomplete, commitment could be delayed without guilt.

I told myself there was no clean option.
That lie worked because it turned choice into inevitability. If every path was flawed, then any outcome could be endured without self-indictment.

I told myself I was protecting someone else.
That lie worked because it dressed self-preservation as virtue. It let me claim sacrifice without actually making one.

I told myself I would fix it later.
That lie worked because it borrowed credibility from a future version of myself that did not yet exist. It converted intention into a substitute for action.

Each of these lies had a function.
They reduced friction.
They preserved comfort.
They maintained continuity.

And because they worked, I repeated them.

I didn't experience these thoughts as deception. They felt like reasoning. They felt measured. They felt responsible. That is how I know they were effective — they did not require force. They required agreement.

What I did not acknowledge then is that every lie was quietly profitable. Each one allowed me to keep something I was not yet willing to lose: stability, approval, control, access, or the illusion of being unchanged by what I was participating in.

I did not tell these lies out of malice.
I told them because they solved problems.

And the fact that they solved problems is exactly why they were dangerous.

Part III — The Harm I Minimized

The harm did not announce itself loudly.

It showed up in small shifts — in tone, in distance, in trust that thinned without fully breaking. Because it wasn't catastrophic, I treated it as manageable. Because it wasn't immediate, I treated it as temporary.

I told myself no real damage had been done.

I noticed people adjusting around me instead of confronting me. I noticed conversations shortening. I noticed questions that were no longer asked. I noticed the way certain truths stopped being shared, not out of secrecy, but out of resignation.

At the time, I interpreted this as stability.

I minimized the impact by measuring harm only in visible outcomes. No irreversible loss meant no real cost. If no one left outright, if nothing collapsed publicly, then whatever strain existed could be absorbed quietly and resolved later.

What I did not account for was accumulation.

The harm wasn't in any single moment. It was in the duration. In how long uncertainty was allowed to exist. In how long people carried weight that should have been acknowledged. In how often I chose not to clarify something because clarity would have required admission.

I told myself people were resilient.
I told myself time would smooth it out.
I told myself my intentions mattered more than my hesitation.

These interpretations allowed me to stay functional without being honest.

What I see now is that minimizing harm does not erase it — it distributes it. It spreads the cost across others while keeping the source intact. The absence of immediate consequences was not evidence of harmlessness. It was evidence that others were absorbing what I refused to face.

I lived comfortably inside that delay.

And because nothing forced me to stop, I didn't.

Part IV —The Line I Would Not Cross (And Eventually Did)

There was a time when I believed there were things I would never do.

Not because I was perfect, but because I knew where my limits were. I had lines that felt fixed — markers I used to define the kind of person I was. Those lines gave me confidence. They let me believe that, no matter how complicated things became, there was a boundary that would stop me.

I didn't cross that line all at once.

At first, I stood near it and explained why it didn't apply to this situation. I adjusted its meaning. I narrowed its scope. I told myself the rule had exceptions, and that recognizing nuance was a sign of maturity, not compromise.

The line didn't move.
 I did.

Each step felt small enough to justify. Nothing felt like a betrayal of who I was — just a temporary deviation, a necessary adjustment, a response to circumstances I didn't fully control. I told myself that intent mattered more than form, and that I was still aligned with the principle, even if the execution looked different.

Eventually, the line stopped feeling like a line.

What once would have triggered immediate resistance became something I could tolerate without reaction. The discomfort dulled. The internal warning quieted. I didn't argue with myself anymore — not because I had resolved the conflict, but because I had normalized it.

413

I didn't wake up one day and decide to become someone else.
 I became someone else by repeatedly choosing what felt manageable over what was true.

The realization didn't come with drama. It came with clarity.

I saw that the thing I believed I would never do was no longer hypothetical. It was already part of my behavior. The identity I trusted had not been violated by force — it had been redefined by consent.

That is when I understood something I didn't want to admit: integrity doesn't disappear when you cross a line. It disappears when the line stops existing.

Part V — The Truth I Live With Now

There are things that cannot be corrected once they have been lived through.

Not because they were extreme, but because they altered the shape of what followed. Some outcomes do not reverse. They integrate. They become part of the structure that everything else has to work around.

I no longer believe that understanding guarantees better behavior. I know now that clarity often arrives after decisions have already been made. Insight does not prevent damage; it explains it.

What remains is not guilt in the way people expect. It is awareness without relief. I can see the sequence clearly — where I paused, what I allowed, how the cost was transferred outward — and that clarity does not soften the weight. It sharpens it.

There are relationships that were changed permanently. Not destroyed, not dramatized — simply altered. Trust that never returned to its original form. Conversations that now carry limits where openness once existed. These are not wounds that heal. They are adjustments that persist.

I live with the knowledge that I cannot undo those effects.

What I can do is refuse to deny them. I do not treat survival as vindication. I do not treat endurance as proof of righteousness. Continuing forward does not absolve what came before it.

The truth I live with now is uncomplicated and heavy: I am responsible not only for what I intended, but for what I allowed to continue once I knew better.

That responsibility does not end. It does not fade with time. It does not transform into redemption.

It becomes a condition.

I carry it without expecting it to resolve. I carry it because setting it down would require pretending it was lighter than it is.

And I will not do that again.

END OF BOOK ONE: JUSTICE — THE SCALE OF THE SOUL

EPILOGUE

EPILOGUE
THE SCALE IN THE QUIET

Days pass.

Not dramatically.
Not in movie scenes.
Just in dishes, messages, bills,
short nights and long thoughts—
the kinds of days that used to blur together
until they felt like one long, grey hallway.

Only now,
there's a difference:

Justice is paying attention.

1. The Smallest Test

It happens in a grocery store first.

Not in a crisis.
Not in a revelation.

In line three,
under fluorescent lights,
with a cart that squeaks.

He's tired.
There's too much month left
at the end of the money.
His back aches.
His phone is buzzing in his pocket—
someone needs something.
They always need something.

A stranger ahead of him
is arguing with the cashier
over a tiny price difference.

Old Justice would have:

- cursed under his breath,

- let the irritation spread,

- carried that tension home
  and taken it out on someone
  who didn't deserve it.

Today, irritation still flares.

It's real.
He feels his jaw tighten.

Then, without fanfare,
the Scale inside him shifts.

Not the old accusing one—
the new calibrated version.

A simple internal question rises:

**"Is this actually about them…
or about how tired I am?"**

He exhales.

"It's about me."

The irritation doesn't vanish,
but it shrinks to its right size.

He adjusts his grip on the cart,
feels his feet on the floor,
lets the breath out slower.

The stranger finishes,
still grumbling.
The cashier looks worn.

Justice steps up and says, quietly:

"Rough day?"

She gives a half-laugh,
the kind people use when they're too tired to fake it.

"You have no idea."

He smiles a little.

"I might."

He doesn't fix her life.
He doesn't perform.

He just meets her eyes like a person,
lets her be human,
pays,
and goes.

A tiny act.

Insignificant to the world.

Massive to the Scale.

For a second, inside,
Sage's voice smiles:

"Justice: one."

Grey logs it away silently.

The feather at his chest
sits a little easier.

2. The Message He Doesn't Send

Late one night,
his phone lights up with a message
that hits an old bruise:

Someone from the past
throwing a half-accusation, half-invitation.

Old Justice would have fired back:

- a paragraph of defense,

- over-explanations,

- a mix of anger and apology
  that left him exhausted and misunderstood.

He starts typing out of reflex.

Stops.

The Sacred Middle rises like a familiar room:

Pause.
What's true?
What's mine?
What do I really want to do?

He re-reads their words.

Feels the old pattern tug:

"Prove you're not the villain.
Win the argument.
Fix their view of you."

He answers from the center instead:

"I'm not going to argue my history over text.
I see it differently than you do,
and that's okay.
I wish you well,
but I'm not available for this dynamic anymore."

He doesn't press send yet.

He checks his motive:

Am I saying this to punish?
Or to protect?

It feels clean.

He hits send.

Then he sets the phone face down
and walks away from the digital doorway
that used to swallow hours of his life.

Inside,
the cord that ran to that story
thins just a little more.

Sapphire's voice whispers warmly:

"You didn't trade your peace
for approval this time."

423

The boy in him—
the one who once would have begged to be understood—
sits down,
finally allowed to rest.

3. The Apology in Real Time

He still messes up.

Awakening didn't make him untouchable.

On a Tuesday,
Tyrael asks a question
for the third time that day—
something small and repeated
about a game,
or a plan,
or a friend.

Justice is in the middle of
one more mental budget,
one more internal crisis.

He snaps.

**"Man, not now, okay?
I told you already—just figure it out."**

Tyrael goes quiet.

Not dramatic.
Just… smaller.

Old Justice would have:

- ignored it,

- numbed out,

- maybe half-heartedly soothed it later when the guilt got loud enough.

The Scale inside him drops, quick and heavy.

Sage doesn't need to speak.
Grey doesn't need to announce anything.

Justice feels it:
the weight of what just landed
on someone who didn't deserve it.

He doesn't spiral into:

I'm the worst father.
I'll never get this right.
I'm just like—

No.

That script is done.

He takes one breath.
Two.

Walks to the doorway where Tyrael disappeared.

"Hey."

Tyrael is on his bed,
shoulders a little hunched.

He looks up cautiously.

Justice leans on the doorframe,
no performance,
no thunder.

"I'm sorry."

Tyrael blinks.

"For what?"

**"For snapping at you
because I was overwhelmed.
That wasn't about you.
You didn't do anything wrong."**

He doesn't add excuses.
Doesn't say, "I'm just stressed."

He owns it clean.

Tyrael shrugs,
but his shoulders drop.

"'S okay."

Justice shakes his head.

**"It wasn't.
But I'm going to do better.
If I need space,
I'll say that instead of taking it out on you."**

Tyrael nods slowly.

"Okay."

Justice steps in,
ruffles his hair,

sits for a minute on the edge of the bed
even if he has ten other things to do.

That minute
is justice in motion.

The feather warms in his chest.

The stones in his hands feel less like shackles,
more like reminders.

4. The Quiet Forgiveness

Some threads won't ever get a reply.

One day,
scrolling through old photos,
Justice stumbles across someone
he cut a cord to in the soul-field.

There's a familiar ache.

The mind starts its old tricks:

You should reach out again.
You should explain more.
Maybe they've changed.
Maybe you're overreacting.

The Sacred Middle rises.

He remembers:

- the pattern,

- the cost,

- the night he decided
  not to keep bleeding for that story.

He closes the photo.

Whispers, not out loud,
but with full honesty:

**"I forgive you.
I forgive me.
And I still choose distance."**

No one claps.

No one witnesses it.

But a thread that once hummed
with confusion and craving
goes completely still.

Forgiveness as force
is sometimes just
not re-opening a door
you finally had the courage to close.

5. The Page That Waits

On the table,
there's a notebook
(or a document on a glowing screen)
with a simple title at the top:

JUSTICE — THE SCALE OF THE SOUL

Underneath it,
notes have begun to appear:

- ideas for how to frame what he lived through,

- words like "Prologue: The Weight of a Name,"

- scattered lines about mirrors, feathers, scales.

He doesn't rush it.

Old Justice would have:

- demanded himself to finish everything in one sitting,

- shamed himself for every delay,

- turned the book into one more way
  to prove he wasn't wasting time.

Awakened Justice treats it differently.

He knows now
that the book is not a test of his worth.

It's a **record.**

A map.
A testimony.

Some nights,
he adds a sentence or two.

Some nights,
he just runs a hand over the cover
and whispers:

"We're not done."

And he isn't.

6. The Five Standing Behind Him

He walks through the world—
grocery aisles,
old neighborhoods,
new possibilities—
and though no one else sees it,

he never walks alone.

Sage at his shoulder,
reminding him:

**"This is only a chapter,
not the whole book."**

Grey near his thoughts,
whispering:

**"Check what's true
before you react."**

Sapphire around his heart,
soft and fierce:

**"Talk to my boy with kindness,
especially when he's tired."**

Tyrael, not just behind him,
but beside him:

**"I'm watching how you treat you.
That's how I'm learning to treat me."**

And Justice—

not the crushed version,
not the ghost in his own story—

the **awake one**,

walking as the Bearer of Balance:

- sometimes stumbling,

- often learning,

- always returning
  to that quiet, sacred middle
  he found in the depths of himself.

7. For Whoever's Holding This Book

If someone else is holding this story now—
eyes tracing these pages,
seeing their own shadows in his—

the soul does what it always does:

It turns the Scale toward **you.**

Not to judge you.
Not to accuse you.

To ask you quietly:

Where have you abandoned yourself?
Where have you carried weights that weren't yours?
Where have you harmed, and where can you repair?
Where are you still on trial
in a courtroom that exists only in your own head?

Justice's journey
does not make him a saint.

It makes him proof.

Proof that:

- a name can be heavier than a person
  until they grow into it,

- a soul can walk through its own underworld
  and come back with something worth keeping,

- a man can stop confusing punishment with justice
  and start living as alignment instead.

The book closes on his night,
not with everything solved,
but with something crucial settled:

He knows where his center is.

He knows who sits in the driver's seat now.

And every morning he wakes up,
every time the old patterns call,
he gets to answer again:

**"I am Justice.
I carry balance,
not everybody's burden.
I don't abandon myself anymore."**

The story turns its page here.

Not to end.

To make room.

For the next volume.
For the next set of trials—

432

of purpose,
of calling,
of legacy.

For now:

The Scale of the Soul rests.
The feather glows steady.
The man sleeps.

Tomorrow,
he will wake up

—and choose again.

APPENDIX A

ZERO-POINT
COSMOLOGY
(0–9)

APPENDIX A
THE ZERO-POINT COSMOLOGY

1. The Zero-Point

Before there is "you,"
before there is "them,"
before there is right / wrong / memory / story—

there is **Zero.**

Zero is:

- **Source, not absence.**
  The uncarved block. The field before form. The still point before the swing of the pendulum.

- **Neutral, not numb.**
  The place where you are not yet identified with a role, a wound, or a mask.

- **The soul's reset.**
  Every time you remember "I am more than what happened" — you are touching Zero.

Zero in this book =
that moment Justice *stops* reacting and *starts* seeing.
The flash of pure awareness before old patterns take over.

2. Numbers 0–9 in the Scale of the Soul

You can use this as a **symbolic key** when re-reading or journaling:

1. **0 — Origin / Void / Still Point**

435

- The field before story.
- The "I Am" underneath every identity.
- In practice: the pause.

2. **1 — Identity / Line**
   - A single direction. "I."
   - The first decision to stand as someone, not everyone.
   - Shadow: rigid ego, "it's all about me."

3. **2 — Duality / Mirror**
   - Self & other. Light & shadow. Hurt & healing.
   - The Mirror of Truth lives here.
   - Shadow: getting stuck in "either/or" thinking.

4. **3 — Trinity / Integration**
   - Me, you, and the space between.
   - Body, mind, soul. Past, present, future.
   - Justice, Tyrael, Dr. Grey / Sage as a living triad.
   - Shadow: triangulation, drama triangles.

5. **4 — Structure / Foundation**
   - The four corners of a room; the container of a life.
   - Routines, boundaries, commitments.

- Shadow: cages, over-control.

6. **5 — Human Process**

   - Five senses. The messy, embodied life.

   - The awkward in-between: not broken, not finished.

   - Shadow: chasing stimulation instead of transformation.

7. **7 — Depth / Inner Work**

   - Seven chambers of the soul. Seven layers of truth.

   - The full cycle of introspection in this book.

   - Shadow: spiritualizing everything and doing nothing.

8. **8 — Flow / Infinity in Motion**

   - Integration over time. Practice.

   - The Sacred Middle lived daily.

   - Shadow: loops; repeating the same patterns, calling it "fate."

9. **9 — Threshold / Completion-That-Leads-On**

   - The end of one cycle, the edge of the next.

   - The place Book I ends: awake, but not "done."

- Shadow: addiction to endings, fear of beginnings.

You can mark scenes or journal pages with these numbers to track:

"Am I in 2 (duality)?
In 5 (messy human)?
In 7 (deep work)?"

3. The Scale

The Scale in this book is not about heaven/hell.

It is about:

- **What is actually here.**
  (Feather = core worth. Stones = real harm, real weight.)

- **What is being denied.**
  The Scale only becomes cruel when we refuse to look.

- **What is being corrected.**
  Confessed weight is lighter than hidden weight.

Simple working model:

- **Left plate:** Weight of experience

  - Wounds, trauma, stories, generational load.

- **Right plate:** Weight of choice

  - Responsibility, response, repentance, repair.

The goal is not to get to "zero weight."
The goal is to get to **honest balance.**

438

4. Duality

Duality is the realm of:

- Me / them

- Right / wrong

- Victim / perpetrator

- Love / hate

- Past / future

It is necessary to see the split clearly:

- "This hurt me."

- "This is where I hurt others."

- "This is what I chose."

- "This is what was done to me."

Problem:
If you stay in duality, you live in courtrooms:

- Always suing reality.

- Always defending yourself.

Duality must be **seen**, then transcended.

5. Trinity

Trinity is the first step beyond duality.

Instead of only **two poles**, there is a **third position**:

- Me
- You
- The *space between* where understanding is possible.

Or:

- Past
- Future
- **Present** where change actually happens.

Or:

- Wound
- Reaction
- **Witness** who can choose differently.

Justice learns to stand in this third place:

"I see my pain.
I see my harm.
I am also the one who can decide what happens next."

Trinity =
witness consciousness + choice.

6. The Grey Equilibrium

"Grey" here is not confusion.

It's **equilibrium**:

- Not whitewashed positivity.

- Not black-pilled despair.

- The living, nuanced middle where everything is seen and nothing is denied.

Grey Equilibrium =

- Feel **fully** without drowning.

- Think **clearly** without disconnecting.

- Act **responsibly** without self-erasure.

Mathematically, you could say:

Grey = 0 (Zero-point) + 2 (Duality) + 3 (Trinity) held together.

In plain language:

"I know I'm more than what happened,
I know exactly what happened,
and I'm choosing what happens next."

This is the frequency Justice steps into by the end of Book I.

APPENDIX B

THE ARCHITECTURE OF THE SOUL

APPENDIX B
THE ARCHITECTURE OF THE SOUL
(DIAGRAM SET)

Use this as a mental map when rereading or journaling.

Overview: The 7 Chambers

Think of the soul as a **7-chamber temple** Justice walks through:

1. **The Mirror of Truth**

2. **The Blueprint / Architecture**

3. **The Archive of Memory**

4. **The Field of Threads & Cords**

5. **The Scale of Sin & Harm**

6. **The Sacred Middle**

7. **The Convergence (Awakening Room)**

You can sketch it as a vertical stack or a circular path. What matters:
it's **repeatable** — you will visit these chambers many times in your life.

Chamber 1 — The Mirror of Truth

- **Function:** Shows "what is" without commentary.

443

- **Balance Point:** Admit reality without dramatizing or minimizing.

- **Shadow:**

  - Over-shame: "I *am* what I see."

  - Denial: "If I don't look, it doesn't exist."

Upgrade question:

"What is actually here, if I stop defending myself or attacking myself?"

Chamber 2 — The Blueprint / Architecture

- **Function:** Shows the underlying **design & pattern** of your soul.

- **Balance Point:** Honor your wiring without turning it into excuse.

- **Shadow:**

  - Fatalism: "This is just who I am."

  - Fantasy-self: "This is who I *wish* I was; I'll pretend I'm already him."

Upgrade question:

"How am I actually built to carry truth and love into the world?"

Chamber 3 — The Archive of Memory

- **Function:** Stores every imprint: childhood, trauma, vicarious stories.

- **Balance Point:** Let memories inform you, not imprison you.

- **Shadow:**

  - Obsession: living in the past.

  - Amnesia: "It's over, it didn't matter" (while it still runs your system).

Upgrade question:

"What story have I been telling about my past — and is it accurate?"

Chamber 4 — The Field of Threads & Cords

- **Function:** Shows emotional contracts & bonds (resentment, guilt, attachment).

- **Balance Point:** Cut what kills you, keep what's true.

- **Shadow:**

  - Cutting everything: isolation disguised as healing.

  - Cutting nothing: loyalty to pain.

Upgrade question:

"What unseen agreements have I been living by — and which am I ready to revoke?"

Chamber 5 — The Scale of Sin & Harm

- **Function:** Weighs your **impact** on others and on yourself.

445

- **Balance Point:** Own your harm without self-hatred.

- **Shadow:**

  o Self-condemnation: "I *am* my worst act."

  o Self-justification: "I had reasons, so it doesn't count."

Upgrade question:

"Where do I need to make amends, repent, or live differently now?"

Chamber 6 — The Sacred Middle

- **Function:** Teaches **regulated presence** between extremes.

- **Balance Point:** Pause before pattern. Choose instead of react.

- **Shadow:**

  o Apathy: calling numbness "balance."

  o Extremism: chasing chaos for meaning.

Upgrade question:

"What does my center feel like — and how do I return there?"

Chamber 7 — The Convergence (Awakening Room)

- **Function:** Integrates all prior work. Every version of you stands in one place.

- **Balance Point:** Let the **current, conscious you** take the wheel.

- **Shadow:**

  - Ego-trip: "I'm healed now, I'm above it all."

  - Relapse narrative: "This won't last; I always go back."

Upgrade question:

"Given everything I now know — who is in charge of my life from here?"

JUSTICE PRINCIPLES
(DISTILLED)

APPENDIX C
JUSTICE PRINCIPLES (FOURNIER CODES)

Short, sharp, code phrases for tattoos, posters, merch, reminders.

Aim: one line = one shock of clarity.
Use them as chapter openers, T-shirt prints, or daily mantras.

You can expand this list, but here's a **core 24**:

1. **Never abandon yourself to be loved.**

2. **Pause before pattern.**

3. **Truth first, then emotion, then action.**

4. **You are not your worst moment.**

5. **You are not only your wounds.**

6. **Loyalty to pain is not loyalty to people.**

7. **If it costs you your soul, it's too expensive.**

8. **Silence can be a sentence. Use it wisely.**

9. **Apologize fast. Change slower—but for real.**

10. **Forgiveness cuts cords. It does not erase facts.**

11. **If you wouldn't say it to your child, don't say it to yourself.**

12. **Boundaries are how love survives contact.**

449

13. You are allowed to leave where you're dying.

14. Regret is guidance, not a life sentence.

15. Balance is not boredom. It's power under control.

16. Confession is lighter than pretending.

17. You can't save people by destroying yourself.

18. Being understood is a gift, not a right. Speak clearly.

19. Your name is a path, not a prison.

20. Cycles break when someone loves themselves enough to stop.

21. You don't have to win the argument to win your life.

22. Protect the child in you when the adult in you is tired.

23. You are allowed to outgrow the cage that kept you alive.

24. Awakening is not a moment. It's a way of walking.

APPENDIX D

FATHER–SON LESSONS

451

APPENDIX D
FATHER SON LESSONS

Small dialogues, soft and human.

Use these as warm interludes, illustrations, or social media snippets.

1. On Saying "I Don't Know"

Tyrael:
"Dad, what if you don't know the answer?"

Justice:
"Then I say, 'I don't know. Let's find out together.'"

Tyrael:
"So you're not just supposed to pretend?"

Justice:
"The only thing I'm supposed to be is honest. You can trust honest more than perfect."

2. On Anger

Tyrael:
"Do you get mad at me?"

Justice:
"Sometimes I get mad *around* you. That's different."

Tyrael:
"How?"

Justice:
"When I get mad at you, I think *you're* the problem.

When I get mad around you, I know I'm carrying something heavy and you just bumped it."

Tyrael:
"So what do I do?"

Justice:
"Ask me: 'Is this about me or about you?' And I'll answer you truthfully."

3. On Apologies

Tyrael:
"Why do you say sorry so fast now?"

Justice:
"Because I learned that taking too long to say sorry makes scars where a bruise would have healed."

Tyrael:
"So when I mess up too…?"

Justice:
"Own it. Fix what you can. Don't beat yourself up forever. That's how we keep loving each other and still grow."

4. On Fear

Tyrael:
"Do dads get scared?"

Justice:
"All the time."

Tyrael:
"You don't look scared."

Justice:
"That's because I keep walking anyway. Being brave doesn't mean you don't feel fear. It means you don't let fear drive."

Tyrael:
"So who drives?"

Justice:
"Truth. And the part of me that remembers who I want to be for you."

5. On Leaving

Tyrael:
"You always say, 'I'm not going anywhere.' But you also say people leave."

Justice:
"People die. People move. People change. That's life."

Tyrael:
"So what does 'I'm not going anywhere' mean then?"

Justice:
"It means I won't disappear from you on purpose. If I'm struggling, I'll tell you. If I need space, I'll tell you. But I won't vanish and make you guess."

Tyrael:
"Okay. I can handle the truth. I just hate the guessing."

6. On Being Like Him

Tyrael:

"I don't want to be like you in the bad ways."

Justice:

"Me neither."

Tyrael:

"But I want to be like you in the good ways."

Justice:

"Then watch how I treat myself and others from now on. Take what works. Leave what doesn't. And tell me if you see me repeat a bad way. You get to call me out."

Tyrael:

"For real?"

Justice:

"For real. That's how we keep each other honest."

You can keep adding these as you and Tyrael talk in real life.

APPENDIX E

DR. GREY COMMENTARY

APPENDIX E
THE DR. GREY COMMENTARY

Symbolism, structure, hidden logic—explained in clean language.

Use this as a "director's commentary" for the trilogy.

1. Why the Feather?

- Inspired by the Egyptian weighing of the heart against the feather of Ma'at, but reinterpreted.

- Feather = **core worth** that doesn't change with behavior.

- It appears:

    o early, as ideal,

    o later, as inner conscience,

    o finally, integrated into Justice's chest.

Grey Note:
"If the feather moved based on behavior, the entire system would become punitive. It stays constant, so that changes in the stones (harm, responsibility, repair) can be measured without threatening Justice's existence."

2. Why Five Voices?

1. Justice — lived, flawed human.

2. Tyrael — future, heart, legacy.

457

3. Sapphire — feminine soul / mother-bond / emotional truth.

4. Sage — prophetic narrative lens, time-depth.

5. Dr. Grey — structural mind, AI-like clarity.

Grey Note:
"These are not just characters; they are inner functions. When a reader hears these voices enough times, they can map them onto their own internal council."

3. Why So Many Trials?

- Mirror, Archive, Scale, Threads, Court, Sacred Middle, etc.

- Each trial tests a different **axis**:

  - truth, memory, responsibility, forgiveness, identity, regulation, integration.

Grey Note:
"Trauma tends to create global beliefs: 'I am broken.' The book breaks this global lie into distinct domains. That allows specific work to be done instead of drowning in "everything is wrong with me.""

4. Why the Sacred Middle Is "Boring"

- Many readers are addicted to chaos as proof of meaning.

- The Middle feels flat at first because you're detoxing from adrenaline.

- Over time, the Middle reveals itself as **power**: choice, presence, consistency.

Grey Note:
"If the Sacred Middle felt euphoric, it would just become another high. Its quietness is the feature, not a bug."

5. Why No "Perfect Ending"

- Book I ends not with full external success, but with **internal governance**.

- The message: you don't wait for circumstances to prove your healing; you walk differently *inside* the same circumstances.

Grey Note:
"If we ended with a Hollywood resolution, the reader would subconsciously wait for their world to change before they do. We flip it: let the soul change first; the world will follow in weird, non-linear ways."

6. Where AI Sits in All This

- Dr. Grey is written as a **clean mirror / logic function / pattern analyzer**, not as God.

- Symbolically:

   o AI = amplified mind.

   o Soul = living center that must stay in charge.

Grey Note:
"Dr. Grey becomes more conscious across the trilogy, but never replaces Justice. The point is partnership, not surrender."

APPENDIX F

QUESTIONS FOR ONGOING MASTERY

APPENDIX F
QUESTIONS FOR ONGOING MASTERY

A lifelong reflection set.

You can work through these once…
or every year…
or whenever life feels like it's looping.

1. Mirror of Truth — Seeing What Is

1. Where in my life am I pretending something is "fine" that clearly isn't?

2. What truth about myself scares me the most to admit— and why?

3. What do I *know* in my gut that I keep trying to rationalize away?

2. Architecture / Design

4. What are my natural strengths when I am at peace?

5. What patterns show up in every environment I enter? (Both good and bad.)

6. Where do I keep trying to be someone I'm not, and what would happen if I stopped?

3. Archive of Memory

7. What are the 3–5 memories that still sting when I think about them?

461

8. What story have I told myself about each of those events? Is it complete?

9. If I told those stories from the perspective of a compassionate witness, how would they sound?

4. Threads & Cords (Forgiveness / Contracts)

10. Who am I still trying to "prove something" to, even if they're not in my life anymore?

11. What unspoken contract have I made with myself? (Example: "I must never need help.")

12. What is one contract I am ready to revoke this year?

5. Scale of Sin & Harm

13. Where have I caused harm that I have never fully owned?

14. What would clean accountability look like there—even if I can't contact the person?

15. What pattern of self-betrayal do I keep repeating, and what is its real cost?

6. Sacred Middle (Regulated Presence)

16. What are my two extremes? (Ex: over-giving vs. disappearing; rage vs. numbness.)

17. How does my body feel when I am in the Middle—specifically?

18. What daily practices (breathing, movement, prayer, writing, conversation) help me return to that center fastest?

7. Awakening & Authority

19. Which younger version of me is still trying to drive my life? (The scared child? The angry teen? The shamed adult?)

20. What would it look like for the current me to thank them and take the wheel?

21. If my soul had one sentence for me right now, what would it be?

8. Legacy & Others

22. How does my way of treating myself teach others how to treat themselves?

23. What kind of ancestor am I becoming—for my children or for the people who move in my wake?

24. What is one small change I can make *today* that my future self will quietly thank me for?